NATIONAL
OBSERVANCE
OF
CHILDREN'S
SABBATHS

Joining
Hearts, Hands, and Voices to Leave No Child Behind®

Worship, educational, community

outreach, and advocacy resources for

Protestant, Catholic, Jewish, and

other faith traditions

2000

Children's Defense Fund

Acknowledgments

Preparation of this manual was supported by the Ford Foundation. All CDF publications are underwritten by the Revson Foundation.

The manual was written and compiled by Shannon Daley-Harris.

Thanks to the following CDF staff for their contributions to this publication:
Anna Rhee, Director of Religious Affairs; Anourack Chinyavong, Designer; Laura Graves, Production Manager; Lisa Clayton Robinson, Editor; Sandra Won, Managing Editor; Helen Blank and Karen Schulman, Child Care Division; Jeannette O'Connor, Child Health Information Project; Kim Adler, Child Watch Division; Debbie Weinstein, Family Income Division; Gigi Hinton, Media Division; Jill Ward, Violence Prevention and Youth Development Project; and Grace Reef, Director of the Intergovernmental Relations Department.

CDF thanks the following contributors who wrote portions of the Children's Sabbath manual:
Walter J. Burghardt, S.J., Coordinator, Preaching the Just Word, Woodstock Theological Center, Washington, DC (Roman Catholic Homily)
The Rev. Ernesto Medina, Missioner for Christian Education, Episcopal Diocese of Los Angeles, Los Angeles, CA (Protestant/Episcopal Sermon and Youth Sermon Preparation Tips)
Rabbi Michael Zedek, Senior Rabbi, Temple B'nai Jehudah, St. Louis, MO (Jewish Sermon)
Margaret Lange, Director of Education, B'nai Jehudah, St. Louis, MO (Jewish Service)
Dr. Siva Subrahmanian, Vice-President, Interfaith Conference of Metropolitan Washington, representing United Hindu Jain Temples, Washington, DC (Hindu Resources)
Amrit Kaur, Secretary, Guru Gobind Singh Foundation, Washington, DC (Sikh Resources)
The Rev. Pat Hoertdoerfer, Director of Children's Programs and Ministries to Families, Unitarian Universalist Association, Boston, MA (Unitarian Universalist Resources and Interfaith Reflection)

In addition, CDF is deeply grateful to the following people for reviewing sections of the manual:
Nancy Joy Allchin, Assistant to the Director, National Spiritual Assembly of Baha'is, Washington, DC (Baha'i Resources)
The Rev. Patricia Daley, Pastor, Hyde Park Presbyterian Church, Hyde Park, MA (Christian Resources)
Mary Alice Gran, Specialist: Ministries with Children, General Board of Discipleship, The United Methodist Church, Nashville, TN (Christian Lesson Plans)
Rabbi Marc Israel, Director of Congregational Relations, Religious Action Center of Reform Judaism, Washington, DC (Jewish Resources)
The Rev. Clark Lobenstine, Executive Director, Interfaith Conference of Metropolitan Washington, Washington, DC (Interfaith Section)
The Rev. Clay Morris, Liturgical Officer, The Episcopal Church, New York, NY (Episcopal Liturgy)
The Rev. Robyn Szoke, Director of Children's Ministries, The Episcopal Church, New York, NY (Episcopal Liturgy)
The Rev. Dr. Susan Willhauck, Lecturer in Christian Formation and Discipleship, Wesley Theological Seminary, Washington, DC (Christian Lesson Plans)

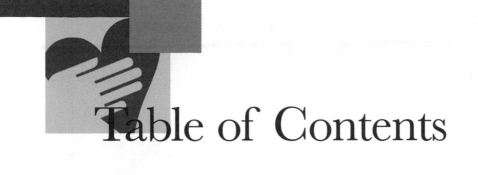

Table of Contents

Please note: Resources for all faiths have a shaded bar along the entire right edge of the page. Resources for Christian congregations have a shaded bar along the top third of the edge, resources for Jewish congregations have a shaded bar along the middle third, and resources for interfaith celebrations have a shaded bar along the bottom third.

A Prayer for Each of Us to Serve

Lord I cannot preach like Martin Luther King, Jr.
or turn a poetic phrase like Jesse Jackson
but I care and am willing to serve.

I do not have Fred Shuttlesworth's and
Harriet Tubman's courage
or Andy Young's political skills
but I care and am willing to serve.

I cannot sing like Fannie Lou Hamer
or organize like Ella Baker and Bayard Rustin
but I care and am willing to serve.

I am not holy like Archbishop Tutu,
forgiving like Mandela, or disciplined like Gandhi
but I care and am willing to serve.

I am not brilliant like Dr. Du Bois or
Elizabeth Cady Stanton,
or as eloquent as Sojourner Truth and
Booker T. Washington
but I care and am willing to serve.

I have not Mother Teresa's saintliness,
Dorothy Day's love or
Cesar Chavez's gentle tough spirit
but I care and am willing to serve.

God it is not as easy as the 60's
to frame an issue and forge a solution
but I care and am willing to serve.

My mind and body are not so swift as in youth
and my energy comes in spurts
but I care and am willing to serve.

I'm so young
nobody will listen
I'm not sure what to say or do
but I care and am willing to serve.

I can't see or hear well
speak good English, stutter sometimes
and get real scared standing up before others
but I care and am willing to serve.

Use me as Thou will to save Thy children today and tomorrow and
to build a nation and world where no
child is left behind and everyone feels welcome.

Marian Wright Edelman, Foreword to *The State of America's Children Yearbook 2000*
(Washington, D.C.: Children's Defense Fund, 2000).

Welcome to the Children's Sabbath

A Letter from Marian Wright Edelman
CDF President and Founder

Dear Faithful Friend:

Beautiful, old quilts hang from the walls of the log building at the Children's Defense Fund-owned former Alex Haley Farm, the spiritual home and leadership development center of the movement to *Leave No Child Behind*. Over the centuries, women have come together to join their hands in crafting such quilts of lasting beauty and warmth.

Today, a friend of mine makes baby quilts for expectant parents she knows. Each quilt is a joint effort. She recruits others who care about the expectant parents and the baby to come – their friends, colleagues, the grandparents-to-be, and college buddies. Each pair of hands sews a different square for the quilt, using a common pattern and materials carefully selected to complement each other. The squares are then joined together, sewn tightly so that the quilt will last through years of being snuggled, dragged, spit up on, and washed. Finally, the finished quilt is presented to the parents and new baby. As it is wrapped around the tiny new one, it represents the union of many hearts and hands on behalf of this new life. It is more beautiful and complete than just one square or just one piece of fabric could have been. It is more meaningful coming from a community of loved ones than a gift from one person alone. It represents love and comfort, protection and hope.

Building the movement to *Leave No Child Behind* in America at this turn of the century and millennium is like that quilt. It is made up of complementary pieces: a Healthy Start, a Head Start, a Fair Start, a Safe Start, and a Moral Start in life and measures to ensure children successful passage to adulthood with the help of nurturing families and caring communities. **A Healthy Start** means that children have healthy bodies and minds, and are assured comprehensive health and mental health coverage and a medical home where they are known. **A Head Start** means that children have strong parents from birth who are supported by communities that truly value families, get the early childhood foundation they need to get ready for school, and high quality schools that inspire, respect, and support every child's success. **A Fair Start** means that children grow up in families with jobs that pay livable wages and are protected from poverty, hunger, and homelessness when parents cannot adequately provide. **A Safe Start** means that children are safe and secure in their homes, neighborhoods, and schools, are protected from the guns that kill a child every two hours, and have safe havens before and after school and during summer months. **A Moral Start** means that parents, other caring adults, and congregations recognize and communicate every child's sacred worth and guide children by example in developing positive, enduring values of justice, compassion, and respect for self and others. Children of all ages need loving limits, discipline, and attention to successfully navigate the paths to adulthood.

Each component is inextricably connected. No piece alone is adequate. Joined together, these pieces promise a comprehensive quilt of protection and care as we strive to *Leave No Child Behind*.

Sadly and unnecessarily, countless children in our nation are not yet wrapped in this quilt of caring concern. More than 11 million children without health insurance are unable to see a doctor when they are sick or to help them stay well. Over 90% of them live in working families. The employed parents of 13 million children who need child care face obstacles of cost, availability, and quality. 13.5 million children are living in poverty that jeopardizes their health, education, dreams, and very lives. Seventy-four percent of them live in working families. Over 4,200 infants, children, and teens were killed by guns in a single year – a classroom full every two days. Five million children are left home alone after school at risk of alcohol and other drug abuse, sexual activity, and crime. And countless children have been left adrift in a culture of materialism, violence, self-gratification, sexism, and racism without enough strong counter voices from parents and other caring adults about the deeper purposes of life.

Just as making a quilt is a joint effort, so too is giving our children the health, educational and moral grounding in life they need. No one person, or sector of our community working alone, can ensure that they are provided. But if we join hearts, hands, and voices as parents, grandparents, friends, religious and community leaders, professionals, and public officials we can.

The Children's Sabbath, too, is like a quilt. No single person can or should do it alone. It should be a team effort of young and old joining together to demonstrate concern for children and faithful commitment to see that no child is left behind. While a Children's Sabbath may focus just on the worship service, some of the most inspiring and effective observances unite worship services, education programs, hands-on service, and advocacy activities, and launch long-term efforts to help children. Each Children's Sabbath should reflect the unique gifts, perspectives, and needs of your congregation and community. And its impact should last for a long time.

I hope that you will join with the Children's Defense Fund in urging your city and our nation to make a positive compact with our children in the 21st century. I also hope you will join with us in making it a reality piece by piece until it is realized. Our 2000-2001 agenda describes the first steps. Please contact us for how you and your congregation and community can help.

I pray that your Children's Sabbath, like a quilt, will be creative and beautiful, that it will unite the hearts, hands and voices of young and old of every faith, race, and income alike, and that it will be a lasting gift that enfolds children in your congregation, community, and our nation in the warm mantle of your love and concern.

In faith,

Marian Wright Edelman

A Compact with America's Children

I. No child shall be hungry in America.
II. No child shall be homeless in America.
III. No child shall lack health care in America.
IV. No child shall be poor in America.
V. No child shall be unsafe in America.
VI. No child shall be illiterate or lack the education and skills needed to work and support a family in America.
VII. No child shall be left alone or in unsafe care when parents work in America.

VIII. No child will be abused, neglected, or exploited for personal or commercial gain in America.
IX. No child will be discriminated against because of race, poverty, gender, sexual orientation, age, or disability in America.
X. Every child will be respected and protected by family, community, state, and nation as a citizen with inalienable rights to life, liberty, and the pursuit of happiness.

A 2000-2001 Action Agenda
to *Leave No Child Behind*®, and to Ensure Every Child a Healthy Start, a Head Start, a Fair Start, a Safe Start, and a Moral Start in Life

At a time of great economic prosperity, a projected $1.9 trillion federal budget surplus over the next decade, and billions of state surplus and tobacco settlement dollars in a post-Cold War era, now is the time to end immoral and preventable child poverty, hunger, homelessness, and sickness in the richest nation on earth. Now is the time to stand up and show our children we truly value them. Now is the time to build a more just and compassionate and less violent society—one where no child is left behind. Together the nation, states, communities, employers, parents, and citizens must:

I. *Ensure Every Child a Healthy Start.* **There are 11.9 million uninsured children in America; 90 percent of them live in working families. Seven million are currently eligible for health care under the Children's Health Insurance Program (CHIP) and Medicaid. Nearly five million are not covered under any program. We must:**

• Mount a massive and urgent campaign to reach and enroll every one of the seven million children now eligible for CHIP and Medicaid.

• Simplify and unify application and eligibility procedures to make it easier rather than harder for children to get health care.

• Expand health coverage to every uninsured child and their parents.

• Encourage employers to expand coverage for employees and their children and stop dropping dependent coverage.

• Urge every community network—religious, health care, parents, senior citizens, education, grassroots, youths, and corporations—to join in a massive and persistent public awareness and enrollment campaign until every child is provided appropriate health care.

II. *Ensure Every Child a Head Start.* **Only 50 percent of children eligible for Head Start and only 10 percent of children eligible for federal child care assistance receive it. Five million school-age children are home alone after school and are at risk of tobacco, alcohol and drug use, teen pregnancy, and violence. Quality preschool, child care, after-school and summer programs, and school systems are essential to getting *all* children ready to learn and achieve and keeping them safe when parents are in the work force.**

• Head Start should be increased to serve one million children in 2000 and all eligible children by 2002, and be expanded to full-day, full-year and to more children under three years old.

- The Child Care and Development Block Grant should be increased by $817 million in 2000 and expanded to reach at least half of all eligible children by 2002.

- Congress should support a new Early Learning Initiative for very young children and significantly increase investments in 21st Century Community Learning Programs and other quality after-school and summer programs.

- Every state should provide a quality comprehensive prekindergarten program for all families who wish to participate and invest more state dollars in quality child care and Head Start programs.

- Every business should offer affordable quality child care, flex-time, and paid parental leave options to help employees balance work and family responsibilities.

- Federal and state family and medical leave laws should be expanded and strengthened to include paid leave.

- Every child should be expected and helped to achieve in quality, equitable school systems.

III. *Ensure Every Child a Fair Start*. Thirteen and a half million children are poor; 74 percent of them live in working families; 5.8 million of them live in extreme poverty in families with incomes below $6,500. They often suffer hunger, homelessness, and lack other basic necessities. A majority of poor children are White and live outside central cities, although over one-third of Black and Hispanic children are poor. Our nation must commit to doing whatever is necessary to end child poverty in America by 2005. Children should get a fair share of the federal and state budget surpluses, tobacco settlement monies, and be guaranteed the same income and health security as senior citizens. We must:

- Ensure work at a decent wage and education and training for parents to improve their job options and earnings.

- Expand the Earned Income Tax Credit (EITC), particularly for families with three or more children, increase the Dependent Care Tax Credit (DCTC) and the Child Tax Credit for lower and middle-income working and stay-at-home parents, and make both credits refundable.

- Make sure that every poor family with children currently eligible for nutrition, health, housing, child care, and other assistance gets them. States should immediately use rather than hoard dollars intended to help parents work and become more self-sufficient, decrease their bureaucracies, and create a culture of service among their employees.

- Strengthen child support enforcement.

IV. *Ensure Every Child a Safe Start*. Over 80,000 American children have been killed by guns since 1979—a greater casualty rate than we suffered in battle casualties in the Vietnam War. American children under 15 are 12 times more likely to die from guns than children in 25 other industrialized nations combined. A child is reported abused or neglected every 12 seconds. Children are exposed to relentless glorification of violence on movie, television, and Internet screens.

- All gun purchasers and owners should be required to register and obtain a license.

- All non-hunting firearms including junk guns and assault weapons should be banned.

- Manufacturers and other adults should be held liable for guns that get into the hands of criminals and children.

- Parents should be educated about the dangers of owning a gun and required to store them locked and secure when they do.

- Cultural leaders, movie, television, and Internet producers, advertisers, and toy manufacturers should stop glorifying and marketing gratuitous violence, which incites some children and youth to violence and desensitizes others to the consequences of violence.

- Nonviolence training, conflict resolution, peer mediation, and other activities to prevent all forms of family violence should be instilled in our homes, congregations, schools, and every sphere of national life.

V. *Ensure Every Child a Moral Start*. It is time for American adults to stop our moral hypocrisy and to live the values we want our children to learn. If we want them to stop being violent, then we should stop being violent. If we want them to be honest, then we should be honest. Parents, preachers, teachers, and all public officials must conduct themselves as they would want their own child or any child to emulate. Private morality and public morality must go hand in hand. Our children need consistent love, time, attention, discipline, family stability, and limits at home and in school, and they need to see that adults in their nation, private sector, and communities value and care for them—not as consumers and future customers to be exploited or as a non-voting group to be ignored—but as the heirs of America's institutions and values. It is time for all adults to accept their responsibility to be good protectors of and mentors for the next generation.

Welcome to the National Observance of Children's Sabbaths!

This year marks the ninth annual celebration of the National Observance of Children's Sabbaths, a weekend of worship, education, outreach, and advocacy that proclaims and responds to the faith-based call to meet the needs of children.

If this is your first time participating in the Children's Sabbath, we are delighted that you are joining in this nationwide movement and trust that you will find it an inspiring and energizing experience for your congregation. If you are a long-time Children's Sabbath participant, we are grateful for your continued witness on behalf of children. Your participation has enriched and strengthened the National Observance of Children's Sabbaths, and will continue to do so.

What is the Children's Sabbath?

The National Observance of Children's Sabbaths is an opportunity for people of all ages and all faiths to learn more about the urgent needs of children and the mandate in every faith tradition to nurture and protect children. Through worship services, religious education classes, and congregational outreach and advocacy activities, people of faith learn more about the problems facing children and commit to responding to them. The goal of the Children's Sabbath is to generate new, long-term efforts to meet children's needs by raising awareness, serving children directly, and advocating on children's behalf.

The Children's Sabbath begins across the nation on Friday with services in synagogues and mosques, and continues through Sunday with church and interfaith worship services. Many Children's Sabbaths are held by individual congregations, while in some communities congregations unite for ecumenical and interfaith celebrations of the Children's Sabbath.

The Children's Sabbath is an intergenerational event that engages people of all ages in planning, participation, and follow-up activities. In this respect, it is different from a traditional "Youth Sunday" that is entirely planned and led by the young people. The focus on serious problems facing children and needed responses also sets it apart from traditional Children's Days.

What is the 2000 Children's Sabbath theme?

The 2000 Children's Sabbath, *Joining Hearts, Hands, and Voices to Leave No Child Behind,* focuses on giving all children the Healthy Start, Head Start, Fair Start, Safe Start, and Moral Start they need and deserve. It addresses the millions of children being left behind without health insurance, in need of quality early childhood and school experiences, in poverty, at risk of violence in their homes, schools, and communities, and adrift without moral guidance and grounding from parents and other concerned adults. The Children's Sabbath affirms the role that parents, congregations, schools, communities, and our nation all have to play in ensuring that no child is left behind.

Although each year the National Observance of Children's Sabbaths has a suggested theme, we hope you will shape that theme to reflect the special concerns of children in your community and congregation.

When is the Children's Sabbath held?

The Children's Sabbath, designated for the third weekend of each October, falls on October 20-22, 2000. If your congregation is unable to celebrate it on this date, however, select an alternate one. What's most important is devoting a time to highlight the needs of children and our responsibility to respond.

Why does the Children's Defense Fund sponsor the Children's Sabbath?

From its inception, CDF has recognized the importance of the faith community's partnership in building a movement to Leave No Child Behind. A nation that lets its children be the poorest citizens has at its heart a spiritual and ethical crisis. Thus, the religious community must help to transform our nation's priorities so that we defend those who are youngest, weakest, poorest, and most vulnerable. For many years CDF worked to support denominations and religious organizations as they developed child advocacy initiatives and campaigns. Eventually, the time was ripe to launch a weekend that would coalesce these efforts into a united moral witness for children that crosses all lines of geography, faith tradition, race, and ethnicity.

Who supports the National Observance of Children's Sabbaths?

The National Observance of Children's Sabbaths is endorsed by more than 200 denominations, faith groups, and religious organizations, and is guided by an Advisory Committee of Jewish, Protestant, Roman Catholic, and interfaith leaders. If you are interested in having your organization become an official endorser of the National Observance of Children's Sabbaths, please call CDF's Religious Affairs Division at (202) 662-3589.

How can I get involved?

Obtaining this manual is the first important step to getting involved in the Children's Sabbath! The next steps are outlined in Section 2: Planning and Promoting Your Children's Sabbath. One of the first decisions you and those who join you in the planning will need to make is whether to plan a Children's Sabbath just for your congregation, or to join with congregations of other faiths or denominations to plan an interfaith or ecumenical Children's Sabbath in your community. (See Section 5 for planning an interfaith service.) Either option is a valuable way to participate. You should determine what is right for your congregation this year.

What's in this manual and how do I use it?

This manual provides planning suggestions, promotion ideas, worship resources, educational programs for all ages, activity ideas, and suggestions for building on your Children's Sabbath to help children throughout the year.

The resources are designed to be easy to use "as is," or they can be adapted to suit your particular congregation. Feel free to use as much or as little as is right for your congregation. Some congregations "put a toe in the water," starting small in the first year and building their celebration in subsequent years; others jump in with both feet right from the start.

We have provided a single manual with resources for Catholic, Episcopal, Jewish, and Protestant congregations, as well as for interfaith celebrations involving many more faith traditions. We hope that you will find the resources for your particular tradition helpful and the other resources enriching.

How have other congregations celebrated the Children's Sabbath?

Although every Children's Sabbath celebration is unique, the best way to understand the Children's Sabbath may be through the inspiring and diverse examples of other congregations' observances and activities in 1999.

- The Children's Sabbath at **Williams Tabernacle Christian Methodist Episcopal Church** in Moultrie, Ga., featured a sermon centered on children's concerns and an act of commitment. The congregation, led by the children, collected toothbrushes for the children's clinic at the Health Department and brought them to the altar during Altar Call. Children who brought toothbrushes received a certificate of appreciation. Their church school hour used the lesson plans provided in the Children's Sabbath manual and had a special closing exercise in honor of the Children's Sabbath using resources from the manual. The church will build on the Children's Sabbath by strengthening their weekday tutorial program, "Homework Hour."

- **Congregation Shir Hadash** in Los Gatos, Calif., focused their second Children's Shabbat on children's safety and gun violence. Speakers at their service included an attorney who is active in the American Jewish Congress (which issued a national call to action demanding tougher gun control), an assemblyman active on child health and education, and a police chief. Information about children and gun violence was distributed, and participants had the opportunity to sign a petition sponsored by the American Jewish Congress calling for meaningful gun control legislation. The service focused on children through prayer and other aspects. To follow up on their Children's Shabbat, the congregation will continue advocating to keep children safe.

- **Mt. Olivet United Methodist Church** in Arlington, Va., heralded their Children's Sabbath with a large yard sign and balloons that let approaching worshipers and passers-by know something special was planned. Their sanctuary was decorated with posters featuring photographs of every child in the congregation in hand-decorated paper "frames." Each church school class wore a particular color shirt, creating a rainbow of children. The prayers, music, and readings were all focused on children's concerns. The children presented a drama as part of the sermon, followed by a short message from one of the pastors. After the service, child-oriented refreshments were served while members signed up to help build a Habitat for Humanity house, purchased note cards to benefit child advocacy organizations and the congregation's own child advocacy committee, and signed up for a four-week parenting course.

- The **Tarrant Area Community of Churches** (TACC) in Fort Worth, Tex., sponsored their eighth interfaith Children's Sabbath, and for the first time held two services in different parts of the county which drew a total of 600 participants. In addition to prayers and readings from the Children's Sabbath manual, the services included a storyteller and music from a number of area children's choirs and a Youth Orchestra. TACC distributed Children's Defense Fund brochures on children and violence, and will build on their Children's Sabbath by joining a new coalition to address the impact of media violence on children.

- **Falls Church Presbyterian Church** in Falls Church, Va., celebrated their Children's Sabbath with a worship service that included prayers, litanies, an act of commitment, and a sermon focused on children. The Sunday School classes used the lesson plans provided in the Children's Sabbath manual. The children drew their pictures on small paper bags that were distributed to the congregation with instructions to fill them with jars of peanut butter and all-fruit jam for a local child care center. To continue the Children's Sabbath commitment throughout the year, the congregation was given a list of a dozen local service and advocacy opportunities (such as "read stories once a week at the Seven Corners Children's Center") with specific contact information to facilitate their involvement.

- **St. Philip's Episcopal Church** in Cincinnati, Ohio, is a small church of 25 members with no children and only one teenager. That didn't stop them from participating in the Children's Sabbath! During their worship service, a retired teacher and former Sunday School

teacher and a lay person in charge of an after-school program addressed the congregation, encouraging them to realize that despite the congregation's size, they can make a big difference for children. To extend the concern of the Children's Sabbath, the congregation will be collecting used children's books for an outreach program, and collecting games for and visiting an after-school program held at the church.

- **Durham's Partnership for Children** in Durham, N.C., encouraged many area congregations to hold Children's Sabbaths by making presentations to interfaith organizations, meeting one-on-one with clergy, mailing letters to congregations, and distributing copies of the Children's Sabbath manual at no cost to faith institutions and community groups. As a result, at least fifty congregations in Durham observed the Children's Sabbath.

For more examples of how congregations have celebrated the Children's Sabbath, visit the Children's Defense Fund's Web site at www.childrensdefense.org, and join CDF's Religious Affairs e-mail network.

Be sure to let us know how *your* congregation celebrates the Children's Sabbath this year! See the Evaluation Form at the end of this manual.

ORGANIZATIONS ENDORSING THE NATIONAL

African Methodist Episcopal Church,
  Women's Missionary Society

African Methodist Episcopal Zion Church,
  Christian Education Department

Akron Area Association of Churches

Alliance of Churches, Ohio

American Baptist Churches U.S.A.

Anti-Defamation League

Antioch Baptist Church

Arizona Ecumenical Council

Arkansas Interfaith Council

Armenian Apostolic Church of America

Arrowhead Council of Churches

Associated Churches of Fort Wayne
  and Allen Counties

Associated Ministries of Thurston County

Baptist Peace Fellowship of North America

Bergen County Council of Churches

B'nai B'rith International

Border Association for Refugees from
  Central America, Inc.

Bread for the World

California Council of Churches

Cape Cod Council of Churches

Carbondale Inter-Church Council

Catholic Archdiocese of Baltimore, Justice and
  Peace Commission

Catholic Archdiocese of Chicago, Office for
  the Ministry of Peace and Justice

Catholic Charities USA

Catholic Diocese of Cleveland,
  Social Action Office

Catholic Diocese of Covington,
  Family Ministry Office

Catholic Diocese of Savannah,
  Office of Black Ministry

Catholic Diocese of Youngstown

Center for Ethics and Economic Policy

Center for Ministry Development

Center for the Prevention of Sexual
  and Domestic Violence

Central Maryland Ecumenical Council

Christian Children's Fund

Christian Church (Disciples of Christ)

Christian Communication Council
  of Metropolitan Detroit Churches

Christian Conference of Connecticut

Christian Council of Delaware and
  the Eastern Shore of Maryland

Christian Council of Metropolitan Atlanta

Christian Methodist Episcopal Church

Church Council of Greater Seattle

Church of Christ in Yale

Church of the Brethren

Church of the Brethren, Atlantic
  Northeast District

Church Women United

Church Women United in Pennsylvania

Churches United of the Quad City Area

Colorado Council of Churches

Community Ministries of Rockville

Congregations Concerned for Children, Child
  Advocacy Network

Congregations Concerned for Children of the
  St. Paul Area Council of Churches

Congress of National Black Churches

Cooperative Metropolitan Ministries

Council of Christian Communions

Council of Churches and Synagogues
  of Lower Fairfield County

Council of Churches, the City of New York

Council of Churches of Greater Bridgeport

Council of Churches of Santa Clara County

Covenant to Care, Inc.

Cross-Lines Cooperative Council

Des Moines Area Religious Council

Dominican Sisters of Edmonds, Wash.

Dominican Sisters of San Rafael, Calif.

Downtown Cooperative Ministry,
  New Haven, Conn.

East Harlem Interfaith, Inc.

Ecclesia: The Ecumenical Mission
  of the Capital Area

Ecumenical Child Care Network

Ecumenical Communication Commission,
  Northwest Ohio

Ecumenical Ministries of Oregon

Episcopal Church Center, Children's Ministries

Episcopal Diocese of Alaska

Episcopal Diocese of Arkansas

Episcopal Diocese of Bethlehem, Pa.

Episcopal Diocese of Los Angeles

Episcopal Diocese of Maryland

Episcopal Diocese of Massachusetts

Episcopal Diocese of Northwestern
  Pennsylvania

Episcopal Diocese of Oregon, Education
  Department

Episcopal Diocese of Pennsylvania, Episcopal
  Church Women

Episcopal Diocese of Southern Virginia

Evangelical Lutheran Church in America,
  Division for Church in Society

Evansville Area Council of Churches

Faith Institute for Black Catholics

Federation of Reconstructionist Congregations
  and Havurot

Florida Council of Churches

For the Love of Children

Franklin Township Ministerial Association

Georgia Christian Council

Grand Rapids Area Center for Ecumenism

Greater Dallas Community of Churches

Greater Flint Council of Churches

Greater Minneapolis Council of Churches

Hawaii Council of Churches

Illinois Conference of Churches

Inner City Renewal Society

Interfaith Center for Faith Action and
  Response of St. Louis

Interfaith Conference of Greater Milwaukee

Interfaith Conference of Metropolitan
  Washington

Interfaith Ministries for Greater Houston

Interfaith Resource Center

International Institute for Islamic Thought

International League of Muslim Women

InterReligious Council of Central New York

Islamic Society of Greater Houston

Jesuit Social Ministries, National Office

Jewish Reconstructionist Federation

Jewish Women International

Leadership Conference of Women Religious

Lexington Theological Seminary

Lincoln Interfaith Council

Lower Bucks Center for Church and
  Community

Lutheran Social Services of Washington
  and Idaho

OBSERVANCE OF CHILDREN'S SABBATHS

Marin Interfaith Council

Metropolitan Area Religious Coalition
  of Cincinnati

Metropolitan Ecumenical Ministry

Metro-Toledo Churches United

Michigan Ecumenical Forum

Minnesota Council of Churches

Mississippi Religious Leadership Conference

Missouri Catholic Conference

Montana Association of Churches

Moravian Church, Northern Province

National Black Catholic Congress

National Committee to Prevent Child Abuse,
  Indiana Chapter

National Council of the Churches of
  Christ in the USA

National Farm Worker Ministry

NETWORK, A National Catholic
  Social Justice Lobby

Network of Religious Communities

New Hampshire Council of Churches

New Jersey Council of Churches

New Mexico Conference of Churches

New York State Council of Churches

North Carolina Conference of Churches

North Dakota Conference of Churches

North Dallas Shared Ministries

North Snohomish County Association
  of Churches

Oak Park–River Forest Community of
  Congregations

Ohio Council of Churches

Ohio–West Virginia YMCA

Parenting for Peace and Justice Network

Pax Christi USA

Peace with Justice Week, National Council
  of the Churches of Christ in the USA

Pennsylvania Council of Churches

Pomona Inland Valley Council of Churches

Presbyterian Child Advocacy Network

Presbyterian Health, Education, and
  Welfare Association

Presbyterian Women in the Presbyterian
  Church USA

Presbytery of Cincinnati

Presbytery of New York City

Rabbinical Assembly

Reconstructionist Rabbinical Association

Reformed Church in America

Reorganized Church of Jesus Christ of
  Latter Day Saints

Rhode Island State Council of Churches

Rochester Area Church Council

Rutgers Presbyterian Church

Sacred Heart School

San Fernando Valley Interfaith Council

San Francisco Interfaith Council

San Francisco Religious Council

Santa Clara Council of Churches

Seventh Day Adventist Church,
  North American Division

Sisters of Charity, BVM, Women's Office

Sisters of the Holy Cross, Notre Dame, Ind.

Sisters of Notre Dame de Namur,
  Chesapeake Province

Sojourners

Solid Ground Ministry

South Carolina Christian Action Council

South Coast Ecumenical Council

St. Paul Area Council of Churches

Tampa United Methodist Centers, Inc.

Tarrant Area Community of Churches

Temple of Understanding

Texas Baptist Christian Life Commission

Texas Conference of Churches

Trenton Ecumenical Area Ministries

Trinity College, Campus Ministry

Tulsa Metropolitan Ministry

Ukrainian Orthodox Church of America

Union of American Hebrew Congregations

Unitarian Universalist Service Committee

United Church of Christ, Connecticut
  Conference

United Church of Christ, Office of Church
  in Society

United Church of Christ, Penn Central
  Conference

United Church of Christ, Penn West
  Conference

United Church of Christ, Southeast
  Association Indiana/Kentucky
  Conference

United Church of Christ, Wisconsin Women's
  Committee

United Methodist Church, General Board of
  Church and Society

United Methodist Church, General Board of
  Global Ministries, Women's Division

United Methodist Church, Harrisburg Area

United Methodist Church, Northern
  Illinois Conference

United Methodist Church, Rhode Island and
  Southeastern Massachusetts District

United Methodist Church, South Carolina
  Conference, Board of Church and Society

United Methodist National Youth Ministry
  Organization, Steering Committee

United Synagogue of Conservative Judaism

Virginia Council of Churches

Voices for Illinois Children

Washington Association of Churches

Washington Ethical Society

West Side Ecumenical Ministry
  of Cleveland

Westside Interfaith Council

Women of Reform Judaism

Women's League for Conservative Judaism

Worcester County Ecumenical Council

World Vision Relief and Development

Wyoming Church Coalition

Planning and Promoting Your Children's Sabbath

This section provides guidelines for planning and promoting a Children's Sabbath celebration in your congregation. See Section 5 for suggestions for organizing an interfaith Children's Sabbath involving congregations of many faiths.

Planning Suggestions for All Faiths

Steps For Planning a Children's Sabbath in Your Congregation:

Begin with prayer. The success of the Children's Sabbath—its ability to stir the hearts and minds and hands of people to nurture and protect children—ultimately relies on God's grace. Seek God's guidance for your Children's Sabbath, turn to God for the strength and commitment to plan it, pray for partners to help you in this venture, and thank God for the precious children God has entrusted to our care. (Those of the Christian faith may want to use the Daily Devotionals provided in Section 3.) Whatever your faith tradition, and whatever words you choose to pray, know that God is with you as you embark on planning a Children's Sabbath.

Secure support from appropriate clergy, staff, or committees. You may find it helpful to show the video *National Observance of Children's Sabbaths: Raising Voices, Linking Hands for Children.* In addition to obtaining approval for planning a Children's Sabbath, do some preliminary investigation into potential sources of financial support for your Children's Sabbath. Of course, you will have a better idea of your budget when you are further into the planning process. You may find that you can plan a Children's Sabbath with little additional expense.

Mark the date on your congregation's calendar. Most Children's Sabbaths will take place on October 20-22, 2000, during a congregation's traditional worship and education time. If your congregation has a conflict with this date, select another. Keeping your celebration during the usual worship time promises greater participation and communicates that the Children's Sabbath is an integral part of your congregation's worship, work, and witness. If you select a time other than your traditional worship hour, be prepared to do lots of extra promotion to ensure a strong turnout.

Recruit a committee to plan the Children's Sabbath and activities leading up to or following it. Involving a broad range of people brings a wealth of gifts and experience, builds greater excitement and "ownership" of the Children's Sabbath throughout the congregation, and helps ensure that no single person gets overloaded. In addition to clergy and congregation staff, consider involving religious education teachers, social action committee members, children and youths, and any interested congregation members. Develop a meeting schedule that will allow sufficient planning time. Many committees find they need more frequent meetings in September and October as the Children's Sabbath draws near.

Identify leadership within the committee.
Designate a chairperson or co-chairs to guide the planning and ensure that goals are set, responsibilities assigned and fulfilled, and that the process moves forward effectively. You also may want to name a secretary who will keep notes of committee meetings and communicate decisions and other information to those involved. (Be sure to keep all who will be affected by Children's Sabbath activities informed, such as musicians, education program teachers and volunteers, and secretaries.) A treasurer could keep tabs on the budget allotted for the Children's Sabbath and also oversee in-kind contributions donated by the community. As the Children's Sabbath planning proceeds, the chairperson/s should assign new tasks and responsibilities as they arise.

Focus your vision for the Children's Sabbath.
What do you hope will happen during and as a result of your Children's Sabbath? Do you want the Children's Sabbath to highlight and affirm the gift and gifts of children? To underscore the responsibility of adults to nurture and protect children? Do you hope to increase awareness about the serious needs of many children today? To broaden the congregation's concern for children to encompass those in the community? Do you want to energize and increase participation in existing congregational programs serving children as a result of the Children's Sabbath? Do you hope to build excitement and commitment for starting a new congregational effort to help children? To stimulate new, individual commitments to giving time or resources to help children? Clarifying your vision for the Children's Sabbath and its impact will help guide your planning for a successful experience.

Determine the format of your Children's Sabbath. You may decide to start small and build your celebration in future years, or you may want to plan an ambitious celebration now. Choose the approach that is right for your congregation and will provide a successful, affirming experience upon which you can build year after year. These are the major components to consider for your Children's Sabbath:

- **Service of worship:** This is the heart of most Children's Sabbath celebrations, lifting up, in prayer, sermon, and song, God's call to people of faith to nurture and protect children. (See Sections 3, 4, and 5 for ideas and resources.)

- **Educational programs:** Educational programs for children, youths, and adults help everyone learn more about the problems facing children, the faith-based call to respond, and ways to make a positive difference. (See Sections 3 and 4 for lesson plans.)

- **Advocacy and hands-on outreach activities:** When people have been inspired and called in the service of worship, and have learned more through the educational programs, they are eager to start making a difference for children right away. Providing concrete outreach and advocacy activities on the Children's Sabbath, perhaps following the service of worship, helps people respond and put their faith into action. (See Section 6 for ideas.)

- **Commitment to longer-term responses to children's needs:** The Children's Sabbath is about more than one weekend a year; it is about inspiring new, long-term responses to the needs of children. Provide opportunities for individuals to find out about, and make commitments to, ongoing action through information tables, presentations, and sign-up sheets. The ongoing action could include participating in existing programs in your congregation, volunteering with a community child-serving program or organization, or even joining a planning committee to develop a new program in your congregation. (See Section 7 for ideas.)

Involve children and youths. The Children's Sabbath is an important time to highlight the gifts, contributions, and leadership of children and youths. However, the Children's Sabbath should not be completely turned over to children, with adults serving only as the advisors and "audience." The Children's Sabbath is meant to be an intergenerational event that demonstrates and celebrates how everyone—children, youths, parents, singles, and seniors—must respond faithfully to God's call to nurture and protect children. (Other occasions celebrated by many congregations, such as Youth Sundays or Children's Day, are more appropriate times to put the service entirely in the hands of children and youths.) Be sure to involve children and youths in the planning process as well as in carrying out parts of the Children's Sabbath. The various sections of this manual offer specific suggestions on how children and youths can participate in promoting the Children's Sabbath, leading the service of worship, and engaging in outreach and advocacy activities. Be sure to solicit young people's ideas and suggestions to supplement those found here.

Involve resource people. After you have determined the basic format and activities for your Children's Sabbath, involve resource people from the congregation and community. These may include health care professionals, public education teachers and administrators, staff of after-school programs, child care providers, Head Start teachers, staff of organizations serving families in poverty, juvenile justice professionals, police officers, staff of community organizations that serve children, elected officials, and representatives of advocacy organizations working on children's behalf. Secular organizations working for children are often eager to find ways to link with religious congregations and draw on the rich resources congregations can offer. Forging these connections will not only assist you in planning your Children's Sabbath weekend, but also should create partnerships for long-term projects that build on the Children's Sabbath.

Recruit volunteers to help prepare for and conduct Children's Sabbath activities. Some who may not have been able to join the ongoing planning committee would welcome responsibility for a specific task in preparation for the Children's Sabbath or on the weekend itself. In addition to recruiting volunteers through personal contact, publicize opportunities through the announcement time in the service, in the congregation's newsletter or bulletin, at meetings, and at gatherings. Tap seniors, children, youths, singles, parents—everyone! The Children's Sabbath is about the role each person can play to nurture and protect children.

Plan to build on the Children's Sabbath. While you are planning the Children's Sabbath, keep your focus on the ultimate goal of stimulating new, long-term congregational and individual commitments to help children year-round. Don't wait until after the Children's Sabbath weekend to think about where you hope it will lead. Instead, make the long-term result of the Children's Sabbath a focus of the planning process. Some Children's Sabbath committees have found it useful to designate a sub-committee on follow-up to begin working on this from the start. (See Section 7 for ideas and resources.) As you plan long-term follow-up, make sure that you involve the necessary clergy, staff, and committees, as well as other interested individuals. Your resource people can also provide input about community needs and opportunities for partnership. Be sure you have a meeting date on the calendar after the Children's Sabbath to convene members of the Children's Sabbath Planning Committee and any others, as appropriate, to move ahead on the follow-up plans.

Take care of "wrap-up" details. After the Children's Sabbath, be sure to attend to details to wind things up. These may include evaluating the Children's Sabbath—what worked, and what you would do differently next time; writing thank you notes to those involved in the leadership and planning and any others who made contributions; marking next year's Children's Sabbath (October 19-21, 2001) on the congregation's calendar; setting a date for the first planning committee meeting (even though the planning committee membership may change); and closing the books on the Children's Sabbath budget. If photographs or videotapes were taken during the Children's Sabbath, you may want to arrange a time to display them to extend the Children's Sabbath experience. Or, begin a scrapbook chronicling your congregation's Children's Sabbaths, and plan to add to it next year.

Mark your calendar!
Next year's Children's Sabbath date:
October 19-21, 2001

Promoting Your Children's Sabbath

Your Children's Sabbath will have the greatest impact if it is effectively promoted and publicized both within your congregation and to the larger community. Here are some ways to do this:

Spreading the Word in Your Congregation

- Place the bulletin insert in this section announcing the Children's Sabbath in your congregation's bulletin or newsletter approximately one month before the date.

- Include other information in your congregation's newsletter. (Adapt the sample congregational newsletter article below.)

- Make posters announcing the Children's Sabbath and display them in the congregation's building. Involve the congregation's youths and children in making these posters.

- Request time to make an announcement during the worship service one or two weeks before the observance.

Reaching Out to the Community and Media

- Show the video *National Observance of Children's Sabbaths: Raising Voices, Linking Hands* to introduce the Children's Sabbath to clergy and interfaith associations, civic groups, and other organizations or associations that may be interested in supporting, attending, or publicizing your Children's Sabbath.

- Mail a letter to civic, social, and religious organizations in your community offering to speak about the Children's Sabbath at their meetings or gatherings. For example, you might contact the PTA, Lions, Rotary, interfaith associations, Boy Scouts and Girl Scouts, and others. Invite them to participate in your congregation's Children's Sabbath or to plan their own Children's Sabbath observance.

- Attend community events such as school open houses, local health fairs, and parades to distribute information about the Children's Sabbath, with permission of event organizers.

- Adapt the sample news release in this section and submit it to the religion page of your local newspaper and to area religious newspapers or newsletters, including denominational publications as appropriate. Follow up with a telephone call to each.

SAMPLE CONGREGATIONAL NEWSLETTER ARTICLE

[Name of Congregation] to Host Children's Sabbath Events

On October 20, 21, and 22, [name of congregation] will join with thousands of other congregations across the nation in the ninth annual National Observance of Children's Sabbaths. Sponsored by the Children's Defense Fund and supported by Catholic Charities U.S.A., the National Council of the Churches of Christ in the U.S.A., the Union of American Hebrew Congregations, and more than 200 other religious organizations and denominations, the Children's Sabbath will focus on the needs of children and on how people of faith can respond through prayer, outreach, and advocacy.

The 2000 national observance theme is *Joining Hearts, Hands, and Voices to Leave No Child Behind*, and will focus on ensuring that every child has a Healthy Start, a Head Start, a Fair Start, a Safe Start, and a Moral Start in life. The Children's Sabbath will encourage all of us—children, youths, parents, single adults, seniors—to become involved in our congregation and local community to assure that no child is left behind and every child has the comprehensive support, nurture, and protection to achieve their God-given potential.

At [name of congregation], we will join in this united voice for children by [describe the events, giving dates and times]. Leading the observance of Children's Sabbath here are [names of several of those who will be involved]. All are invited. This will also be a good time to invite other families or children to visit our congregation. For more information, contact [name and phone of contact person in the congregation].

- If you have any contacts who know a columnist for the local paper, solicit their help in pitching the Children's Sabbath to the columnist.

- Contact your local radio station to learn the requirements and formats for having your Children's Sabbath events publicized as a Public Service Announcement (PSA) or on its community calendar or community bulletin board. You may be asked to prepare a live read script—a brief (10 seconds) script giving the basic information. For example: "[Name of congregation] located at [cross streets or address] is planning a special celebration and events on [date] to involve young and old in responding to the urgent needs of children. For more information, call [name of congregation]. Your heart, hands, and voice are needed to help children at risk." Type it, double-spaced, with accurate names, times, and addresses. Be sure to include your name as a contact for the station, with daytime and evening phone numbers. Send it to the station at least two weeks in advance.

- Invite the local media—television, radio, and print—to attend and publicize the Children's Sabbath. Tell them about aspects of the events that promise to be interesting and emotionally compelling. Point out that the Children's Sabbath is a way to focus attention on serious problems facing children and on positive ways to make a difference. Let them know about any well-known speakers who will be participating in your Children's Sabbath.

- Arrange for a local spokesperson or an interfaith panel of speakers to participate on a radio or television talk show program about an issue of concern for the children in your community.

- If your community has a cable or public access television station, contact the station's producers to arrange an interview. Ask if they will also air the Children's Sabbath video.

- Write a letter to the editor about the urgency of acting to see that we leave no child behind and give every child a Healthy Start, a Head Start, a Fair Start, a Safe Start, and a Moral Start in life. Offer the Children's Sabbath as a way to learn more and become involved. Watch the newspaper for articles about children's health, early childhood development, poverty, violence, or children in general, so that you can relate your letter to those articles and time it appropriately.

News Release for Local Media

One of the goals of the National Observance of Children's Sabbaths is to reach a wider, secular audience with a message of children's needs and the religious community's concern and commitment to meeting those needs. We encourage you to use the following sample news release as a model for explaining the Children's Sabbath to your local newspaper's religion or community news editor and as a means of generating a news story. Here are steps to follow:

1. *Call* your newspaper to obtain the name of the religion writer or city editor. If you know someone who works for the newspaper or has contacts there, ask for his or her help in getting the news release into the right hands.

2. *Mail* the news release to the right person at the paper in early October, two to three weeks before your Children's Sabbath.

3. *Follow up with a telephone call* a few days later. Remember, the news media are looking to cover a newsworthy story, not to promote a particular event. In your communication with them, emphasize that the Children's Sabbath is about children's issues of concern to many people and is a practical and inspiring example of how people are taking action. Emphasize that your celebration is part of a growing national movement among religious congregations to Leave No Child Behind. Suggest that reporters contact the Children's Defense Fund's Media Division at 202-662-3609 for background information and a national perspective to supplement your own.

4. *Send a letter of thanks* to the reporter if the paper does cover your story, with copies to superiors. Building and maintaining a good relationship with the religion writer or other reporter may help gain coverage of follow-up efforts developing from your Children's Sabbath and of the Children's Sabbath in subsequent years.

5. *Send a copy* of any coverage you receive to the Religious Affairs Division of the Children's Defense Fund to assist in further promotion of the Children's Sabbath.

[For more information and ideas on media work, see *How Shall They Hear? A Handbook for Religious Communicators* from the Religious Public Relations Council (an Interfaith Association of Religious Communicators), published by Mission Communications. $14.95 plus $5 shipping and handling. Call 1-800-947-0207].

SAMPLE NEWS RELEASE

FOR IMMEDIATE RELEASE
October 18, 2000

[YOUR CONGREGATION'S NAME] JOINS THE CHILDREN'S DEFENSE FUND IN CELEBRATION OF THE NATIONAL OBSERVANCE OF CHILDREN'S SABBATHS

[Name of your town, state]—[Your congregation's name] will be holding a special worship service on [date and time] to draw attention to the needs of our nation's children. [Your congregation's name] is one of thousands of churches, synagogues, mosques, and other places of worship around the nation celebrating the Children's Sabbath this weekend as part of the Children's Defense Fund (CDF)'s annual observance. The National Observance of Children's Sabbaths started 9 years ago and seeks to enlist congregations and religious organizations to work on behalf of children through prayer, service, and advocacy. This year's theme is "Joining Hearts, Hands, and Voices to Leave No Child Behind."

"The Children's Sabbath is an opportunity for religious congregations to come together on behalf of all of our children," said Marian Wright Edelman, Founder and President of the Children's Defense Fund. "No one person, or sector of our community working alone, can give our children the health, educational, and moral grounding in life they need. But if we join hearts, hands, and voices as parents, grandparents, friends, religious and community leaders, professionals, and public officials, we can."

Congregations of many faiths will be responding to the call to action throughout the weekend of October 20-22, with special worship services, activities, religious education programs, and special events. Many will make long-term commitments to help children.

"We are proud to be part of this national effort," said [your congregation's religious leader's name]. "We hope the community will join us and that the light we shine will be a beacon of hope and recognition for our children to know they are cherished and cared for."

For more information about [your congregation's name]'s celebration of the Children's Sabbaths, contact [contact person's name, title, group affiliation, telephone number, and e-mail address, if available].

Reproducible Resources for All Faiths

The following pages provide several resources that may be photocopied. No additional permission is needed.

Children's Sabbath Clip Art (pages 19-22)

Reproduce the images on these pages to enhance your newsletter, worship bulletin, flyers, posters, letters, and other materials related to the Children's Sabbath.

Announcement Bulletin Insert (pages 23-24)

This bulletin insert announces to members of your congregation your plans to participate in the 2000 Observance of Children's Sabbaths. Fill in the appropriate date, time, and contact information. Photocopy these two pages back to back on 8¹/²" x 11" paper, and cut down the middle to make two bulletin inserts per photocopy. Distribute this bulletin insert a month before your Children's Sabbath to alert congregation members and build excitement and participation.

Children's Sabbath Service Bulletin Insert (pages 25-26)

This bulletin insert is to be used on the day you celebrate the Children's Sabbath. Photocopy this insert on both sides of 8¹/²" x 11" paper. Fold in the middle so that "Joining Hearts, Hands, and Voices" appears at the top of the front page and "How Can We Serve?" appears on the back.

If you are able, compile a list of specific ways that congregation members can serve by volunteering with or donating to community or congregation-based programs serving children, with local contact information. Substitute that list for the more general suggestions under "How Can We Serve?"—type it to fit in the same space, put it in place of the existing section, and photocopy it as part of the bulletin insert.

Clip Art

LEAVE NO CHILD BEHIND ®

LEAVE NO CHILD BEHIND ®

LEAVE NO CHILD BEHIND ®

Joining Hearts, Hands, and Voices to Leave No Child Behind ®

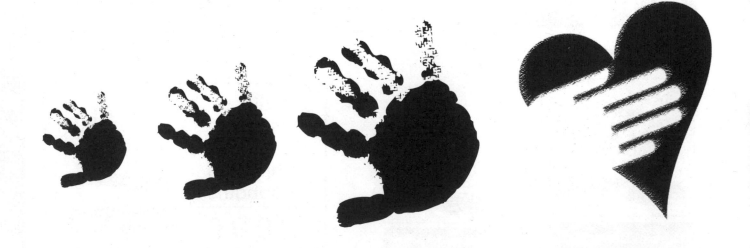

Clip Art (continued)

Clip Art (continued)

Joining Hearts, Hands, and Voices to Leave No Child Behind®

The ninth annual National Observance of Children's Sabbaths—October 20-22, 2000—will join people of all ages and faiths in making a commitment to Leave No Child Behind and to give every child a Healthy Start, a Head Start, a Fair Start, a Safe Start, and a Moral Start in life.

Beginning with services in synagogues and mosques on Friday and concluding with church and interfaith services on Sunday, thousands of congregations across our nation will join in the Children's Sabbath through prayer, worship, religious education classes, special hands-on service activities, and advocacy efforts. They will learn more about the problems facing children, reflect on the faith mandate to respond, and make new commitments to Leave No Child Behind.

Our Congregation Plans to Participate!

Date: _____

Time: _____

To learn more about what our congregation is planning and how you can become involved, contact: _____

Joining Hearts, Hands, and Voices to Leave No Child Behind®

The ninth annual National Observance of Children's Sabbaths—October 20-22, 2000—will join people of all ages and faiths in making a commitment to Leave No Child Behind and to give every child a Healthy Start, a Head Start, a Fair Start, a Safe Start, and a Moral Start in life.

Beginning with services in synagogues and mosques on Friday and concluding with church and interfaith services on Sunday, thousands of congregations across our nation will join in the Children's Sabbath through prayer, worship, religious education classes, special hands-on service activities, and advocacy efforts. They will learn more about the problems facing children, reflect on the faith mandate to respond, and make new commitments to Leave No Child Behind.

Our Congregation Plans to Participate!

Date: _____

Time: _____

To learn more about what our congregation is planning and how you can become involved, contact: _____

Today, countless children are being left behind. More than 11 million children without health insurance aren't getting a **Healthy Start** in life. The obstacles of cost, quality, and availability mean that some of the 13 million preschoolers cared for by someone other than their parents aren't getting a **Head Start**. The five million children left home alone after school aren't getting a **Head Start** either. The 13.5 million American children living in poverty aren't getting a **Fair Start** in life. The children gunned down at a rate of one every two hours in our nation aren't getting a **Safe Start**. And countless children adrift in a culture of materialism, racism, violence, and self-concern without the guidance and support of parents and other caring adults, congregations, and communities aren't getting a **Moral Start** in life.

On the Children's Sabbath, we will join our hearts, hands, and voices to see that no child is left behind. Together, we can work faithfully to give all children the start in life they need and deserve.

> Let your work be manifest to your servants,
> and your glorious power to their children.
> Let the favor of the Lord our God be upon us,
> and prosper for us the work of our hands—
> O prosper the work of our hands!

(Psalm 90:16-17)

Today, countless children are being left behind. More than 11 million children without health insurance aren't getting a **Healthy Start** in life. The obstacles of cost, quality, and availability mean that some of the 13 million preschoolers cared for by someone other than their parents aren't getting a **Head Start**. The five million children left home alone after school aren't getting a **Head Start** either. The 13.5 million American children living in poverty aren't getting a **Fair Start** in life. The children gunned down at a rate of one every two hours in our nation aren't getting a **Safe Start**. And countless children adrift in a culture of materialism, racism, violence, and self-concern without the guidance and support of parents and other caring adults, congregations, and communities aren't getting a **Moral Start** in life.

On the Children's Sabbath, we will join our hearts, hands, and voices to see that no child is left behind. Together, we can work faithfully to give all children the start in life they need and deserve.

> Let your work be manifest to your servants,
> and your glorious power to their children.
> Let the favor of the Lord our God be upon us,
> and prosper for us the work of our hands—
> O prosper the work of our hands!

(Psalm 90:16-17)

Joining Hearts, Hands, and Voices to Leave No Child Behind®

n the Children's Sabbath and throughout the year, people of faith are joining their hearts, hands, and voices to Leave No Child Behind and see that all children—gifts from God—have the start in life they need and deserve. Through prayer, hands-on service, and advocacy, congregations will be putting their faith into action to Leave No Child Behind.

National Observance of Children's Sabbaths

2000

DEAR LORD, BE GOOD TO ME THE SEA IS SO WIDE AND MY BOAT IS SO SMALL

Children's Defense Fund®

How Can We Serve?

Hold children in your heart: Pray for the children being left behind. Pray for guidance to know how best you can help. Pray for the strength and commitment to make a difference in children's lives.

Extend a helping hand: Commit to one specific act of compassion to help a child who is being left behind, whether it is a one-time activity or a new, long-term commitment. Volunteer with or donate to a congregation-based or community program serving children, or look for a need that no one is meeting right now.

Lift your voice for justice for children: Write a letter to your members of Congress and state elected officials about the needs of children and urge them to demonstrate leadership in solving them. Write a letter to the editor of your local newspaper responding to articles about children's concerns. Urge positive, concerted action to address children's needs. Attend community meetings on children's needs and ask a question or offer a solution. Join in a rally on children's concerns.

Prosper for us the work of our hands—
O prosper the work of our hands!

Today and every day, countless children in America are left behind.

The children needing a healthy start:
- 1,540 babies are born without health insurance.
- 798 babies are born at low birthweight, weighing less than 5 lb. 8 oz.

The children needing a head start:
- 13 million children are in child care, yet in one four-state study, only one center in seven received a rating of good quality care.
- Nearly five million children are left home alone after school each school day.
- 2,806 high school students drop out each school day.

The children needing a fair start:
- 2,140 babies are born into poverty.
- 547,000 children are in foster care.
- 11.8 million children rely on food stamps for their meals.

The children needing a safe start:
- Nearly 12 children and youths under age 20 die from firearms.
- Over 100,000 children are in detention, correctional, or shelter facilities.

The children needing a moral start:
- 218 children are arrested for violent crimes.
- 399 children are arrested for drug abuse.
- 5,044 children are arrested.

Together, we can work faithfully to give every child the start in life they deserve.

A Healthy Start means that children have healthy bodies and minds, and are assured a comprehensive health and mental health system that provides preventive care when they are well and treatment when they are ill.

A Head Start means that children have strong parents from birth who are supported by communities that truly value families, get the early childhood foundation they need to get ready for school, and attend high quality schools that inspire, respect, and support every child's success.

A Fair Start means that children grow up in families with jobs that pay livable wages and are protected from poverty, hunger, and homelessness when parents cannot adequately provide.

A Safe Start means that children are safe and secure in their homes, neighborhoods, and schools, are protected from the guns that kill a child every two hours, and have safe havens before and after school and during summer months.

A Moral Start means that parents, other caring adults, and congregations recognize and communicate every child's sacred worth and guide children by example in developing positive, enduring values of justice, compassion, and respect for self and others. Children of all ages need loving limits, discipline, and attention to successfully navigate the paths to adulthood.

3

Christian Worship and Education Resources

T his section provides worship suggestions and resources for Christian congregations, as well as liturgies specifically for Roman Catholic parishes, Episcopal parishes, and Protestant churches. It also contains sermon resources, a children's sermon, a children's activity bulletin, and a seven-day devotional guide that may be photocopied and distributed to members on the Sunday preceding Children's Sabbath. Finally, it includes lesson plans for all ages.

Worship Suggestions

- **The week before the Children's Sabbath, distribute copies of the Daily Devotional Guide on pages 49-52 to help congregation members prepare their hearts and minds for the Children's Sabbath.**

- **During the Children's Sabbath, distribute the bulletin insert on pages 25-26 in this manual and the children's activity bulletin on pages 53-54 in this manual.**

- **Use or adapt one of the sample worship services provided in this section.**

- **Create your own materials on the theme of children and the need for action.**

- **Use readings from worship and prayer books that include a social action theme.**

- **Incorporate resources from your denomination that focus on children and child advocacy.** For example, the Presbyterian Church (USA) has a *Vision Statement* on ministry to children, The Episcopal Church has an *Episcopal Charter for Children*, the Evangelical Lutheran Church in America has a *Safe Haven for Children* program, The United Methodist Church uses *The Bishops' Initiative on Children and Poverty*, and the Roman Catholic Church has the Bishops' statement *Putting Children and Families First: A Challenge for our Church, Nation*

and World. These could be used in place of a more traditional affirmation of faith, used as an act of commitment, or incorporated into another part of the service.

- **Select hymns and anthems that focus on children and our responsibilities to them.** The sample worship services in this section include music suggestions.

- **Focus the sermon or homily on children and our responsibility to act on their behalf.** The sermon resources on pages 40-45 are based on the Gospel lesson designated in the Revised Common Lectionary, Roman Catholic Lectionary, and Episcopal Lectionary for October 22, 2000.

- **Use or adapt the suggested Children's Sermon on page 46.** Or, in a role reversal, have one of the children give an "Adults' Sermon"— a short message from a child addressed to adults.

- **Invite a youth to deliver the sermon.** See page 47 for suggestions on coaching youth sermon preparation and delivery.

- **Commission staff and board members of child-serving programs affiliated with the congregation,** and celebrate their work as part of the congregation's mission.

- **Invite every adult to pray throughout the year for a particular child in the church.** Possibilities include distributing photographs of the children so the adults have visual reminders of the children for whom they are to pray, asking the children to fill out index cards (noting their name, parents, grade, and something about themselves) that are then distributed to adults who will pray for them, or simply printing the name of a different child at the top of every bulletin.

- **Invite a speaker from a program serving children to deliver a "minute for mission"** during your announcement time or to speak at another point in the service. Encourage the speaker to highlight opportunities for members to become involved themselves and to speak out for children.

- **Collect a special offering to benefit a program serving children or families,** such as an after-school program, mentoring and tutoring program, community health clinic, or Head Start program. Announce the offering in advance so that members will be prepared. Dedicate the offering during the service. The offering could be in the form of money or items such as children's books, baby food, or diapers.

- **Invite on-site child care or Head Start staff, administrators, parents, and children to attend your Children's Sabbath.**

Involve Children and Youths. The Children's Sabbath, unlike a traditional Youth Sunday or Children's Day, is intended to involve adults in the planning and leadership of the day. As members of the congregation, adults must recognize the challenges facing children in our nation, and their collective responsibility to respond. However, the Children's Sabbath is an important time to include children and youths in the planning and leadership of the worship service and all other events.

For example, children and youths can:

- Have an overnight "lock in" at the church beforehand to learn about worship and plan their parts in the Children's Sabbath.
- Design and paint the paraments (such as the cloth draping the pulpit).
- Draw pictures for the bulletin cover.
- Decorate the sanctuary with drawings or banners they have made. A number of congregations adorn their sanctuaries with photographs of the churches' children. Hang the photographs from fishing line or glue them onto poster board.
- Assist and greet worshipers as they arrive or leave, light candles, or collect the offering.
- Begin the Children's Sabbath by entering in a procession. The children could carry a banner they made.
- Read prayers and scriptural passages and lead responsive readings.
- Write a prayer to be used in the service.
- Present a short drama or liturgical dance as part of the service.
- Sing a special anthem, play an instrumental piece, or perform a song in sign language.
- Remain throughout the entire service instead of departing for church school classes. If the children remain throughout, ensure that the worship service appropriately engages them.
- Be "adopted" by adults to sit together during the service.

Catholic Liturgy

Joining Hearts, Hands, and Voices to Leave No Child Behind

Sunday, October 22, 2000

This sample liturgy provides suggestions for incorporating the focus of the National Observance of Children's Sabbaths into the standard liturgy for the 29ᵗʰ Sunday in Ordinary Time, Year B. [All hymn numbers refer to Worship, *GIA Publications.]*

Introductory Rites

Entrance Song: "Lord of Our Growing Years" (#556), "There's a Spirit in the Air" (#531), "Gather Us In" (#665), or "God Is Here! As We His People" (#667)

Greeting

In the name of the Father, and of the Son, and of the Holy Spirit.
Amen.
The grace of our Lord Jesus Christ and the love of God and the fellowship of the Holy Spirit be with you all.
And also with you.

We gather on this day to worship God and to celebrate God's gift of children and God's call to nurture and protect them. We join with congregations of many faiths across our nation in the ninth annual National Observance of Children's Sabbath. Together we will work faithfully to put children and families first and leave no child behind.

Penitential Rite

Priest: Coming together as God's family, with confidence let us ask the Father's forgiveness, for he is full of gentleness and compassion.

Lord Jesus, you are the good shepherd who has laid down your life for your sheep:
Lord, have mercy.

People: Lord, have mercy.

Priest: It is not the will of your Father in heaven that one of these little ones should be lost:
Christ, have mercy.

People: Christ, have mercy.

Priest: Lord Jesus, you commanded us to feed your lambs:
Lord, have mercy.

People: Lord, have mercy.

Priest: May almighty God have mercy on us, forgive us our sins, and bring us to everlasting life.

People: Amen.

Gloria

Opening Prayer

Almighty and ever-living God, our source of power and inspiration, give us strength and joy in serving you as followers of Christ, who lives and reigns with you and the Holy Spirit, one God, for ever and ever. **Amen.**

Liturgy of the Word

First Reading: Isaiah 53:10-11

Responsorial Psalm: Psalm 33 (#955)

Second Reading: Hebrews 4:14-16

Gospel Acclamation

Priest: Alleluia.

People: Alleluia.

Priest: Whoever becomes humble like this child is the greatest in the kingdom of heaven. (Mt. 18:4)

People: Alleluia.

Gospel: Mark 10:35-45

Homily
(See Sermon Resources in this section.)

Profession of Faith: The Nicene Creed (or Apostles, per *Directory for Masses with Children*)

General Intercessions (Prayer of the Faithful)

My brothers and sisters, through this common prayer, let us pray to our Lord Jesus Christ, not only for ourselves and our own needs, but for all people, young and old, near and far. Let us pray, saying "Lord, bless the children."

For the holy Church of God, that we more closely follow the steps of your Son who came to serve and blessed the children, we pray to the Lord.

Lord, bless the children.

For all the peoples of the world, especially the children dying from preventable illness and malnutrition, denied educational opportunity, stunted by poverty, scarred by warfare, and questioning their worth, we pray to the Lord.

Lord, bless the children.

For our nation and our leaders, that we put children and families first, giving every child a healthy start, a head start, a fair start, a safe start, and a moral start in life, we pray to the Lord.

Lord, bless the children.

For ourselves and our community, that we discover greatness in serving children and those most in need, we pray to the Lord.

Lord, bless the children.

For all the children, that they bloom in good health and flourish in loving care, that they know sufficiency and share their bounty, that they walk in ways of peace and know themselves loved by God, we pray to the Lord.

Lord, bless the children.

For all who have died, especially the children who died from lack of health care, poverty, violence, and suicide, we pray to the Lord.

Lord, bless the children.

God, who embraces us as beloved children, hear the prayers of your Church, and grant us today what we ask of you in faith. We ask this through Christ our Lord. **Amen.**

Liturgy of the Eucharist

Preparation of the Altar and the Gifts

Offertory Song: "For the Beauty of the Earth" (#557)

Prayer Over the Gifts

Lord God,
may the gifts we offer
bring us your love and forgiveness
and give us freedom to serve you with our lives.
We ask this in the name of Jesus the Lord.

Eucharistic Prayer

Communion Rite

The Lord's Prayer

Doxology

Sign of Peace

Breaking of the Bread-Agnus Dei

Communion

Communion Song: "Draw Us In the Spirit's Tether" (#731)

Song of Praise: "Lord Whose Love in Humble Service" (#630), "Jesu, Jesu, Fill Us With Your Love" (#431), or "The Church of Christ in Every Age" (#626)

Prayer After Communion
Let us pray.
Lord,
may this eucharist help us to remain faithful.
May it teach us the way to eternal life.
Grant this through Christ our Lord. **Amen.**

Concluding Rite

Greeting
The Lord be with you.
And also with you.

Blessing
May almighty God bless you,
the Father, and the Son, and the Holy Spirit.
Amen.

Dismissal
Go in peace to love and serve the Lord.
Thanks be to God.

Concluding Hymn: "Our Father, by Whose Name" (#570)

Episcopal Liturgy

Joining Hearts, Hands, and Voices to Leave No Child Behind

Sunday, October 22, 2000

This sample liturgy provides suggestions for incorporating the focus of the National Observance of Children's Sabbaths into the standard Episcopal liturgy for Proper 24, Year B, which falls on October 22, 2000. Throughout the liturgy, we have provided two options, one from The Book of Common Prayer *and the other from* Enriching Our Worship: Supplemental Liturgical Materials *prepared by The Standing Liturgical Commission of The Episcopal Church. The following material has been reviewed and approved by the office of the liturgy for The Episcopal Church. (Where noted, hymn suggestions are from* Wonder, Love, and Praise: A Supplement to The Hymnal 1982 [WLP]; *otherwise, hymns are from* The Hymnal 1982.*)*

The Word of God

Hymn: "God is Love, and Where True Love Is" (#576) or "Here, O Lord, Your Servants Gather" (#792, *WLP*)

Opening Sentences

Option 1:

(From *The Book of Common Prayer*, hereafter referred to as *BCP*)

Celebrant	Blessed be God: Father, Son, and Holy Spirit.
People	And blessed be His kingdom, now and forever. Amen.

Option 2:

(From *Enriching Our Worship: Supplemental Liturgical Materials* prepared by The Standing Liturgical Commission, hereafter referred to as *EOW*)

Celebrant	Blessed be the one, holy, and living God.
People	Glory to God forever and ever.

Celebrant may say

Almighty God, to you all hearts are open, all desires known, and from you no secrets are hid: Cleanse the thoughts of our hearts by the inspiration of your Holy Spirit, that we may perfectly love you, and worthily magnify your holy Name; through Christ our Lord. Amen.

Song of Praise: "Now Thank We All Our God" (#396), "Joyful, Joyful, We Adore Thee" (#376), "We Will Extol You" (#404), or "O Threefold God of Tender Unity" (#743, *WLP*)

The Collect of the Day

Option 1: *(BCP)*

Celebrant	The Lord be with you.
People	And also with you.
Celebrant	Let us pray.

Proper 24 *(BCP)*

Almighty and everlasting God, in Christ who came as a child you have revealed your glory among the nations: Preserve the works of your mercy, that your Church throughout the world may persevere with steadfast faith in the confession of your Name; through Jesus Christ our Lord, who lives and reigns with you and the Holy Spirit, one God, for ever and ever.

People Amen.

Option 2: *(EOW)*

Celebrant	God be with you.
People	And also with you.
Celebrant	Let us pray.

On the Children's Sabbath

Gracious and almighty God, source of all love and justice: Help us on this Children's Sabbath to hear your call to care for the children. Strengthen our hands and embolden our hearts that we may act with your love and speak with your justice, to the end that no child will be left behind and every child will have the start in life that you intend; through Jesus Christ our Lord, who lives and reigns with you and the Holy Spirit, one God, for ever and ever.

People Amen.

The Lessons

A Reading from Isaiah 53:4-12

Option 1: *(BCP)*
After each reading, the Reader may say
The Word of the Lord.
People   Thanks be to God.

Option 2: *(EOW)*
After each reading, the Reader may say
Hear what the Spirit is saying to the churches.
People   Thanks be to God.

Gradual Hymn: "You Who Dwell in the Shelter of the Lord" (#810, *WLP*)

A Reading from Hebrews 4:12-16

Gospel Announcement

Option 1: *(BCP)*
The Holy Gospel of our Lord Jesus Christ, according to St. Mark.
People   Glory to you, Lord Christ.

Option 2: *(EOW)*
The Holy Gospel of our Savior Jesus Christ, according to St. Mark.

Gospel: Mark 10:35-45
(See High School Lesson Plan for a scripted dramatic reading of this passage.)

After the Gospel, the Reader says
The Gospel of the Lord.
People   Praise to you, Lord Christ.

The Sermon
(See Sermon Resources in this section.)

The Nicene Creed

The Prayers of the People
(Alternative Prayers of the People may be found in the Catholic Liturgy and Protestant Service.)

With all our heart and with all our mind, let us pray to the Lord, saying "Lord, bless the children."

For the Universal Church, that we more closely follow the steps of your Son who came to serve and blessed the children, let us pray to the Lord.

Lord, bless the children.

For our nation and our leaders, that we put children and families first, giving every child a healthy start, a head start, a fair start, a safe start, and a moral start in life, let us pray to the Lord.

Lord, bless the children.

For children everywhere, especially the children dying from preventable illness and malnutrition, denied educational opportunity, stunted by poverty, scarred by warfare, and questioning their worth, let us pray to the Lord.

Lord, bless the children.

For ourselves and our local community, that we discover greatness in serving children and those most in need, let us pray to the Lord.

Lord, bless the children.

For all the children, that they bloom in good health and flourish in loving care, that they know sufficiency and share their bounty, that they walk in ways of peace and know themselves loved by God, let us pray to the Lord.

Lord, bless the children.

For those who suffer, especially the millions of children in our rich land who live in poverty, lack health care, and are wounded by violence, let us pray to the Lord.

Lord, bless the children.

For all who have died in the hope of the resurrection, and for all the departed, especially the children who died from lack of health care, poverty, violence, and suicide, we pray to the Lord.

Lord, bless the children.

We pray to you also for the forgiveness of our sins.

Leader and People:
Most merciful God,
we confess that we have sinned against you
in thought, word, and deed,
by what we have done,
and by what we have left undone.

We have not loved you with our whole heart;
we have not loved our neighbors as ourselves.
We are truly sorry and we humbly repent.
For the sake of your Son Jesus Christ,
have mercy on us and forgive us;
that we may delight in your will,
and walk in your ways,
to the glory of your Name. Amen.

Absolution

Option 1: *(BCP)*
The Bishop when present, or the Priest
Almighty God have mercy on you, forgive you all your sins through our Lord Jesus Christ, strengthen you in all goodness, and by the power of the Holy Spirit keep you in eternal life. *Amen.*

Option 2: *(EOW)*
Almighty God have mercy on you, forgive you all your sins through the grace of Jesus Christ, strengthen you in all goodness, and by the power of the Holy Spirit keep you in eternal life. *Amen.*

The Peace

The Celebrant says to the people
Let us share the peace of Christ with one another, and give thanks for the children among us who show us new ways to walk in peace together.

Option 1: *(BCP)*
Celebrant The peace of the Lord be always with you.
People And also with you.

Option 2: *(EOW)*
Celebrant The peace of Christ be always with you.
People And also with you.

The Holy Communion

Offertory: "Lord Make Us Servants of Your Peace" (#593), "What Does the Lord Require" (#605), "The Church of Christ in Every Age" (#779, *WLP*), or "Lord, You Give the Great Commission" (#780, *WLP*)

(You may wish to include the Act of Commitment, found in the Protestant Service, as a way for parishioners to make an offering of themselves—their time, commitment, voices.)

The Great Thanksgiving

Option 1:
Eucharistic Prayer B *(BCP)*

Proper Preface for Children's Sabbath
Because you gave your own Child, Jesus Christ, to reveal the fullness of your love which leaves no one behind and embraces us all as your beloved children

Option 2:
Eucharistic Prayer for the Children's Sabbath
Celebrant The Lord be with you.
People And also with you.

Celebrant Lift up your hearts.
People We lift them to the Lord.
Celebrant Let us give thanks to the Lord our God.
People It is right to give our thanks and praise.
Celebrant We give you thanks, living and loving God, for calling our world into being— for making earth and water, plants and animals, and then for making each and every one of us in your image— every woman and man, every girl and boy, of every race and place, rich and poor.

We give you thanks for loving each of us as a mother loves her children, for promising to be our God no matter what— welcoming us as a father even when we have done wrong.

On this Children's Sabbath day, we thank you especially for children, for the ways they are eager to learn and for the things that they teach us, for the challenges that don't stop them and for the successes they celebrate, for the way in which each one is wonderfully made, a gift from you. And so we join the saints and angels in proclaiming your glory, as we sing (say),

Celebrant and People Holy, holy, holy Lord, God of power and might, heaven and earth are full of your glory. Hosanna in the highest. Blessed is the one who comes in the name of the Lord. Hosanna in the highest.

The Celebrant continues We praise you, O God, You sent your beloved child Jesus to enter our world as a baby, to grow as a child in mind and body, to teach others that God loves us as a parent, to hug the children close and bless them, to tell all people that it is only by being like a child that we may enter God's reign, to heal children and adults who were sick in their bodies, minds, and hearts, to be a friend to people who were poor, looked down upon, left out by others.

Jesus went even to the cross that we
may know your love, triumphant even
over death,
that frees us to live as your
beloved children.

*At the following words concerning the bread, the
Celebrant is to hold it, or lay a hand upon it;
and at the words concerning the cup, to hold or
place a hand upon the cup and any other vessel
containing the wine to be consecrated.*

On the night before he died for us, Jesus
was at table with his friends. He took
bread, gave thanks, broke it, and gave it
to them, and said: "Take, eat: This is my
Body, which is given for you. As you do
this, remember me."

As supper was ending, Jesus took the
cup of wine.

Again, he gave thanks, gave it to them,
and said: "Drink this, all of you: This is
my Blood of the new Covenant, which is
poured out for you and for all
for the forgiveness of sins. Whenever
you drink it, remember me."

Around your table, as your children,
O God, we remember Jesus Christ, who
came in love, lived in love, and died in
love, who was and is and is to come. We
offer to you our gifts of bread and wine,
and we offer to you our lives.

Pour out your Spirit upon these gifts that
they may be for us the Body and Blood
of Christ, that they strengthen us to
welcome the children, to show your love,
to work for your justice.

Through Christ and with Christ and in
Christ, in the unity of the Holy Spirit, to
you be honor, glory, and praise, for ever
and ever. *AMEN.*

The Lord's Prayer

The Breaking of the Bread

Option 1: *(BCP)*
Alleluia. Christ our Passover is sacrificed for us;
Therefore let us keep the feast. Alleluia.

Option 2: *(EOW)*
We break this bread to share in the Body of Christ.
We who are many are one body, for we all share in the one bread.

Communion Hymn: "Lord, Whose Love Through
Humble Service" (#610), "Jesu, Jesu, Fill Us With Your
Love" (#602), "Take My Life, and Let It Be" (#707), or
"I, The Lord of Sea and Sky" (#812, *WLP*)

Post Communion Prayer

Option 1: *(BCP)*
Let us pray.
Eternal God, heavenly Father,
you have graciously accepted us as living members of
your Son our Savior Jesus Christ, and you have fed us
with spiritual food in the Sacrament of his Body and
Blood. Send us now into the world in peace, and grant
us strength and courage to love and serve you with
gladness and singleness of heart; through Christ our
Lord. Amen.

Option 2: (adapted from *EOW*)
God of abundance,
you have fed us with the bread of life and cup
of salvation;
you have united us with Christ and one another;
and you have made us one with all your people in
heaven and on earth.
Now send us forth in the power of your Spirit,
that we may proclaim your redeeming love to the
world through serving the children whom you created
and love—
and continue forever in the risen life of Christ our
Savior. Amen.

The Blessing *(EOW)*

The Wisdom of God
the Love of God
and the Grace of God
strengthen you
to be Christ's hands and heart in this world, in the name
of the Holy Trinity. Amen.

The Dismissal

Celebrant	Remembering especially all our children, let us go in peace to love and serve the Lord.
People	Thanks be to God.

Protestant Service of Worship

Joining Hearts, Hands, and Voices to Leave No Child Behind
Sunday, October 22, 2000

This service provides a model for incorporating the focus of the National Observance of Children's Sabbaths into a Protestant service. It should be adapted as appropriate to conform to your congregation and denomination. It draws on the texts designated in the Revised Common Lectionary for the 29th Sunday in Ordinary Time, Year B (October 22, 2000). Congregations that do not follow the Revised Common Lectionary or that are celebrating the Children's Sabbath on an alternate date may wish to substitute different texts.

Call to Worship

(The reading from Matthew 18 could be read in parts by a narrator and "Jesus," or it could be accompanied by a silent enactment.)

Leader 1: Then little children were being brought to him in order that he might lay his hands on them and pray. The disciples spoke sternly to those who brought them; but Jesus said, "Let the little children come to me, and do not stop them; for it is to such as these that the kingdom of heaven belongs." (Matthew 18:13-14)

Leader 2: God welcomes each one of us here today, young and old, confident and doubting, rich and poor, women and men. Together, let us praise the One who extends loving arms of welcome and blessing to us.

Hymn of Praise: "God is Here!"

Call to Confession

We are ever in need of God's grace, from our first days to our last.

Jesus knows our every weakness,
and loves us still!
Because we have faith in him,
we dare to approach God with confidence.
Let us confess our sin before God and one another.

Prayer of Confession

God of great and small, we confess that we succumb to desires for success on the world's terms. We begin to think that biggest, strongest, most popular, and richest is best. In our race to get ahead, we trample on people and principles, and leave our children behind.

Help us to remember your concern for the smallest and weakest, the outsiders and those who are poor. Help us slow down and listen to our children, listen to our hearts, listen for your word. Remind us that being first and fastest isn't most important. Guide us to serve others, especially the children who are being left behind.

Assurance of Pardon

Hear the good news! God sent Jesus that we may know ourselves to be loved and forgiven children of God. Rejoice in God's love!

Sung Response: "Jesus Loves Me!"

The Peace

Hymn: "Make Me a Channel of Your Peace"

Prayer for Illumination

Gracious God, help us to listen for your word to us today
with the openness and trust of a child
with the questioning mind of a youth
with the discerning heart of one grown to maturity
with the wisdom of one seasoned by years.

First Reading: Job 38:1-7 (34-41)

Second Reading: Hebrews 5:1-10

Anthem/Hymn: "The Church of Christ in Every Age"

Gospel Reading: Mark 10:35-45

(If the children will be remaining throughout the service instead of departing for church school classes, you may wish to present the Gospel reading in a dramatic enactment. See The High School Lesson Plan for a script.)

Sermon

(See Sermon Resources in this section.)

Hymn: "Jesu, Jesu, Fill Us With Your Love"

Affirmation of Faith

(Select one from your tradition that most closely relates to the day's theme.)

Other Liturgical Responses to the Word

(According to your tradition, one or more of the following may be incorporated into the service: Baptism, reaffirmation of baptismal vows, or other pastoral rite of the Church.)

Prayers of the People

Leader: In Jesus, we do have one who knows our weaknesses, who knows our needs, who came as servant and friend to bring healing where we need it most. Let us turn to God in prayer.

For all babies, especially babies born too soon and too small, for sick and injured children without health care, for parents who bear the double pain of a sick child and the inability to afford care,

People: Lord, grant them a healthy start.

Leader: For all children, especially children whose bright promise is squelched in poor quality child care, for children denied the opportunity of Head Start, for children and youths whose schools may teach failure and discouragement,

People: Lord, grant them a head start.

Leader: For all children, especially children bearing the brunt of poverty, with hungry tummies and heavy hearts, for parents who work hard at jobs that still leave them below poverty and unable to provide their families' basic needs,

People: Lord, grant them a fair start.

Leader: For all children, especially children who cower under beds fearing bullets outside their windows or beatings inside their homes, for youths whose fear, despair, and anger lead them to carry guns and plan their funerals, for parents who see their children slipping into trouble and don't know what to do,

People: Lord, grant them a safe start.

Leader: For all children, especially children who don't know their inherent, God-given worth, for youths abandoned to find their own values who turn to peers and media to measure self-worth, for parents who long to guide their children but wonder if it is too late,

People: Lord, grant them a moral start.

Leader: With God, it is never too late for us. God offers us fresh beginnings every day, the chance to find the new start we need, the opportunity to provide a new start for a child. Thanks be to God. **Amen.**

The Eucharist

(Congregations that will be celebrating the Lord's Supper should include the appropriate liturgical material. See also the Episcopal Liturgy.)

Act of Commitment

Leader: God calls us, not just this day but every day, to nurture and protect children whom God has entrusted to our care. God has given each of us gifts and skills to use for the well-being of children. Let us commit to reach out and care for children...wipe a tear, bandage a scraped knee or comfort a scraped heart, tutor a struggling student, paint over graffiti, plant a community garden, become a foster parent, provide an internship, coach a sports team, hold a hand...whatever you hear God calling you to do.

People (sing):
Take my life, and let it be consecrated, Lord, to thee.
Take my moments and my days; let them flow in ceaseless praise.
Take my hands, and let them move at the impulse of thy love.
Take my feet, and let them be swift and beautiful for thee.

Leader: Our God calls us to do justice, and to speak out for those who cannot speak. Let us commit to being voices for justice, proclaiming God's concern for those who are young, weak, and poor. Let us find ways to support children's causes with our time, talents, and treasures.

People (sing):
Take my voice, and let me sing always, only, for my King.
Take my lips, and let them be filled with messages from thee.
Take my silver and my gold; not a mite would I withhold.
Take my intellect, and use every power as thou shalt choose.

Leader: As we serve and speak out for children, may we be guided and sustained by the one who came to us as servant and advocate. Let us rely on prayer and the believing community to keep our vision faithful, our hearts loving, and our commitment steady.

People (sing):
Take my will, and make it thine; it shall be no longer mine.
Take my heart, it is thine own; it shall be thy royal throne.
Take my love, my Lord, I pour at thy feet its treasure-store.
Take myself, and I will be ever, only, all for thee.

(For a reproducible version of the words and music to
"Take My Life, and Let it Be," turn to page 112.)

Hymn: "Lord Whose Love Through Humble Service"

Charge and Blessing

Let us go forth
to love, serve, and seek justice
for all of God's children.

Now, may the God who
watches over us
came for us and
works through us
be with you, beloved children of God. Amen.

Alternative Blessing, Sung (Away in a Manger, v. 3):
Be near us Lord Jesus;
we ask you to stay
close by us forever
and love us we pray.
Bless all the dear children
in Thy tender care,
And fit us for heaven
to live with Thee there.

Additional Worship Resources

Call to Worship

Leader: In the presence of a God whose word has called the earth and the stars into being,
Unison: We stand in awe.
Leader: In the presence of a God whose arms have held children,
Unison: We stand in trust.
Leader: In the presence of a God whose breath has stirred within us and caused our hearts to thirst for justice,
Unison: We stand in need.
Leader: Before you, Giver of Life, we come in faith, in search of love and justice and wholeness.
Unison: Be with us; hear us, we pray. Amen.

(from *More Than Words*)

Call to Worship

Come, O People!
Sing and rejoice for this is Children's Sabbath.
With glad and thankful hearts we shall praise God.
With what shall we come before God?
What will be pleasing to God?
We come with a passion for justice and mercy.
We would walk faithfully with God.
Listen and you will hear the most wonderful story about Jesus' great love for children.
We are eager for the story and want to make it our own.
We would love the children as Jesus loves us.

(by the Rev. Jon Schultz)

Call to Worship

Whose world is it?
The world and all that is in it belong to the Lord;
The earth and all who live on it are God's.
Let us worship our God whose will is justice and peace, and who calls us to act with justice, to love mercy and kindness, and to walk without pretense, arrogance, or prejudice—humbly with our God.

¿De quien es el mundo?
El mundo y todo lo que hay en el pertenece al Señor;
la tierra y todo lo que habita en ella pertenece a Dios.
Adoremos a nuestro Dios cuya voluntad es la justicia y paz, y que nos llama a actuar con justicia, a amar misericordia y bondad, y a andar sin pretensión, arrogancia o prejuicio—humildemente con nuestro Dios.

사 회 자 : 누구의 세계인가 ?
회 중 : 세계와 그 안에 모든 것이 주의 것이요.
          이땅과 그 위에 모든 것들이 하나님께 속했네.

사 회 자 : 그의 뜻이 공의로우신 하나님을 예배하세.
          그는 우리도 하여금 공의를 행하시고
          자비와 인자도 사랑하며 겸손이 거치대와
          오만과 편견이없이 그와 동행하길 원하시네.

(from the 1991 Churchwide Gathering of Presbyterian Women)

Prayer of Confession

Lord, we have pushed so many of our children into the tumultuous sea of life in leaky boats without survival gear. Forgive us and help them to forgive us. Help us now to give all our children the anchor of faith, the rudder of hope, the sails of education, and the paddles of family to keep them going when life's sea gets rough. Amen.

(by Marian Wright Edelman)

Prayer of Confession

We confess, O God, that we struggle with ourselves;
we allow our fears and inadequacies
to keep us from caring for others
whose lives are even more fragile than our own;
we speak of seeking peace with justice,
but are content with the peace of solitude,
the injustice of silence,
sometimes because we just cannot see
how we might make a difference.
Yet in a small vulnerable child,
You gave us a Savior;
in fleeting tender moments
You make us Your own.
Forgive us, and show us O God,
what we may do together to find Your peace.

(by Diana C. Austin)

Assurance of Pardon

This is the Good News which Christ makes known to us:
We are forgiven!

> Because we are forgiven,
> > we have peace to share;
> because we are loved enough,
> > we have love to give;
> because we are touched by God's mercy,
> > we have grace to share;

Thanks be to God!

(by Diana C. Austin)

Renewal of Commitment

Leader: The Lord, our God, gives us peace.
People: May we be the instruments of God's coming.
Leader: The Lord, our God, gives us hope.
People: May we be the channels of God's promise.
Leader: The Lord, our God, gives us power.
People: May we be the means of its initiation.
Leader: The Lord, our God, gives us justice.
People: May we be the keepers of its vigil.
Leader: The Lord, our God, trusts us.
People: May our covenant be sealed in obedience and expectation.
Leader: Through Christ our Lord.
People: Amen.

(from *Banquet of Praise*)

Prayer

Lord, think Your thoughts in us
do Your work through us
build Your peace in us
share Your love through us. Amen.

(by Marian Wright Edelman, adapted)

Sending Prayer

God of power,
may the boldness of Your Spirit transform us,
may the gentleness of Your Spirit lead us,
may the gifts of Your Spirit equip us
to serve and worship You now and always.

Dios de poder,
que la osadia de tu Espiritu nos transforme,
que la dulzura de tu Espiritu nos dirija,
que los dones de tu Espiritu nos capaciten
ahora y siempre.

(from *In Spirit and In Truth*, worship book for the 1991 World Council of Churches, Canberra.)

Sermon Resources

To help you prepare the sermon or homily for the Children's Sabbath, we have provided several resources:

• two sample homilies/sermons, one by the Rev. Walter J. Burghardt, S.J., Coordinator of the Preaching the Just Word Project of Woodstock Theological Center, and one by the Rev. Ernesto Medina, Missioner for Christian Education of the Episcopal Diocese of Los Angeles. Both are based on Mark 10:35-45, which is the Gospel reading in the Revised Common, Episcopal, and Roman Catholic Lectionaries for October 22, 2000. Seeing how others have linked the text designated by their traditions to the themes and concerns of the Children's Sabbath may spark your reflection, provide new insights, inspire your writing, and open your eyes to new connections.

• a sample Children's Sermon, for a special time with children during your service.

• suggestions for coaching young people's preparation of the sermon, if you decide to have a youth preach on the Children's Sabbath.

Stories and Statistics About Children:

Integrated throughout this Children's Sabbath manual are stories about children who are being left behind, quotes from children, and statistics that document the crises they face. You may want to use these as a resource for sermons, prayers, newsletter articles, and other aspects of your Children's Sabbath.

Stories About and Quotes From Children:
Sample Catholic Children's Sabbath Homily (pages 41-43)
Adult Lesson Plan ("Children Today Are Being Left Behind") (pages 73-74)
Sample Jewish Sermon (pages 86-87)
Jewish Service (pages 79-85)

Statistics About Children:
A Letter from Marian Wright Edelman (pages 3-6)
Bulletin Inserts for All Faiths (page 26)
Sample Catholic Children's Sabbath Homily (pages 41-43)
Middle School Lesson Plan ("Put Yourself in Their Shoes") (page 65)
High School Lesson Plan ("Sound Bite Facts") (page 67)

No Child Left Behind: A Call To Every Christian

Sample Children's Sabbath Homily by
Walter J. Burghardt, S.J., Coordinator of the Preaching the Just Word Project,
Woodstock Theological Center, Washington, D.C.

On the wall of my office in Washington, D.C., I have taped a photograph. It is a picture that meets my eye each time I enter, and often when I leave. It shows a young boy, perhaps ten years old, barely five feet high. He is standing in the middle of a gigantic garbage dump somewhere in Brazil. His cap, on backwards, half covers a mop of filthy hair. His face is almost hidden behind dirt and soot; his eyes stare at me unblinking; his mouth is closed tight, the ends of his lips down, sullen. His hands are stuffed into the pockets of pants that will never be clean again. His shoes are all but planted in mud. This is where he works. He is a scavenger. He collects used paper, plastics, rags, and bottles from garbage dumps and sells them to retailers for recycling. It is among the most hazardous of jobs, destructive of health as well as of hope.

I grace my wall with this photo because the mud-caked Brazilian boy is not alone. He compels me to listen, forces me to hear the world's children crying—yes, even America's children, children who have no lobby comparable to tobacco and the gun. He will not let me go until I plead with the followers of Christ to heed the anguished cry of the Children's Defense Fund and the Children's Sabbath, "Leave No Child Behind!" Actually, it is not so much me who pleads; it is the Christ who demanded that we let the children come to him "because it is to such as these that the kingdom of God belongs" (Mt.10:14).

A lovely thought, but what does this mean in down-to-earth living? Five practical suggestions. For every child, five "starts."

I

First, a Healthy Start. In the richest country on earth 13.5 million children are living in poverty. Not the genteel poverty of the child Jesus in Nazareth. If you are poor in the U.S., the odds are stacked against you before you are born: You have less chance of being born healthy, even surviving. Your physical growth is stunted; you are more likely to be neglected or abused; your resilience and emotional reserves wear down. Any hopes you have are crushed.

Yes, poverty even kills. Low-income children are two times more likely than others to die from birth defects; three times more likely to die from all causes combined; four times more likely to die in fires; five times more likely to die from infectious diseases and parasites; six times more likely to die from other diseases.[1]

These are not simply secular statistics to be deplored. These are God's children, God's creation, crying to the privileged to live like the Christ we claim to follow, the Christ who "came not to be served but to serve," who gave his "life as a ransom for many" (Mk. 10:45). What can, what ought, a Christian to do? Get to know one family in your area that is living below the poverty line. Are the children insured? Immunized? Do they have untreated illnesses, injuries, chronic health conditions? Do they know about CHIP, the Children's Health Insurance Program, available in all 50 states and the District of Columbia? Persuade your parish to shape a massive effort to uncover and deal with the health of the poor.

"Let the little children come to me."

Continued on page 42

Continued from page 41

II

S econd, a Head Start. Among the gifts our good God has designed for us is a share in one of God's own prerogatives: the awesome power to know. To leap over oceans with the speed of light and touch different cultures. To stare at the stars and be awed by the wonder of God's creation. To make sense out of words on a page, pictures on a wall, ideas in a mind. To look into another's eyes and realize you are not alone, you are loved. To read God's own Book and discover that God's Son took your flesh, walked your earth, died for you.

God's design, yes; but millions of our children are deprived of all this. Why? Poverty, hunger, one-parent homes, illness, inadequate schools, "killing fields" for their environment. In 1994, 40 percent of fourth-graders (69 percent of Blacks, and 64 percent of Hispanics) could not read at a basic level.[2] For millions, a college education is an impossible dream.

What can we do? Get involved. On a parish level, if possible. In any case, personally. Realize that the public school is not the enemy of the parochial. It is our Catholic concern when a half million students drop out every year. Our Catholic concern, because a school is not a building; it is a child, it is these children, living fearfully in a world they cannot understand.

Some enchanted evening, fold a little stranger in your arms—tell him a story, read with her, and open a new world, a Disneyland of delight. Bring laughter to eyes that rarely sparkle.

"Let the little children come to me."

III

T hird, a Fair Start. It means that children grow up in a situation that is genuinely a community, caring of one another, concerned. You see, when our imaginative God fashioned woman and man, far from God's mind were innumerable individuals scattered haphazardly over a globe, basically independent of one another. God had in mind a human family, a single community, bound together not by race or income but by love.

In point of fact, today we rarely have a city or town that is a genuine community. For the most part we have three communities. There are the highly prosperous: no economic problems. There are the impoverished, living below the poverty line. And there is the middle class, once fairly secure, now anxious about how to make ends meet even with a generous salary. There is a tremulous truce between the haves and the have-nots, the African American and the Caucasian—yes, between the "poor whites" and the prosperous.

Again it is the children who suffer most dreadfully. In America, the younger you are, the poorer you are. Our children need both parents, and yet a 1996 study predicted that by 2001, 50,000 children and youths (to age 21) would be orphaned by AIDS in New York City alone.[3] Do I know any of these children, any of these parents? Poor parents need jobs that pay a living wage. If their jobs don't, should we not suggest to some that they take advantage of the federal Earned Income Tax Credit to help support their children? My point is, these people need *community* support: your support and mine, your parish and mine.

"Let the little children come to me."

IV

Fourth, a Safe Start. Guns kill a child every two hours. In my own backyard, the District of Columbia, over 200 children were killed by gunfire in a single five-year period. In consequence, many of D.C.'s children are preparing not their futures but their funerals—where to be waked, how to look, how to be dressed. They do not expect to live very long. And the killings that have ravaged schools in the past several years have transformed our halls of learning into high-security areas. Again, not cold statistics. Each of these boys and girls was once a vibrant person, a child of God, beloved of God.

Not ours to patrol the streets or the schools. But dare we, dare any one of us, declare "Guns are not my problem"? Only a concerted community effort can effectively confront the powerful gun lobby. Not to banish guns altogether; only to make it extraordinarily difficult for potential killers to buy them.

"Let the little children come to me."

V

Fifth, a Moral Start. Healthy and educated, cared for and safe—all important if a child is not to be left behind. Important, but not quite enough. Each child must absorb and develop a core system of values, so as to grow into a person genuinely human. A value system that, at its best, includes a real relationship to God in knowledge and love; respect for every other man, woman, and child as a person; and reverence for the earth that sustains us in existence. It demands as an intimate feature a special concern for the less fortunate, the downtrodden, the ailing, the helpless, the stranger, the different, the immigrant, the refugee. This calls for collaboration between parents and school and church (or synagogue or mosque).

It will not be easy. Parents are not always there, and if there, not always helpful. Public schools are limited by law in the morality they may communicate. Churches are increasingly seen by the young as spiritual cafeterias from which one chooses what one likes at the moment. And still, the young reveal an enthusiasm, a yearning for self-giving, an openness to dedicated, imaginative models that with God's promised grace can mature a child in the image of the Christ who lived and died for others.

"Let the little children come to me."

What has all this to do with Catholic Christians? Simply this: We are not followers of Jesus if we do not take to ourselves the declaration of Jesus, "Whoever wishes to be first among you must be slave of all. For the Son of Man came not to be served but to serve, to give his life" for others (Mk 10:45). I beg you, my sisters and brothers, let the little children come to him.

---

1. Marian Wright Edelman, Introduction to Arloc Sherman, *Wasting America's Future: The Children's Defense Fund Report on the Costs of Child Poverty* (Boston: Beacon, 1994), xvii.
2. See *The State of America's Children Yearbook 1999* (Washington, D.C.: Children's Defense Fund, 1999), p. 75.
3. See ibid. p. 88.

REFLECTIONS FOR THE NATIONAL OBSERVANCE OF CHILDREN'S SABBATHS

Sample Children's Sabbath Sermon by the Rev. Ernesto R. Medina, Missioner for Christian Education, Episcopal Diocese of Los Angeles

James and John, the sons of Zebedee, came forward to him and said to him, "Teacher, we want you to do for us whatever we ask of you." And he said to them, "What is it you want me to do for you?" And they said to him, "Grant us to sit, one at your right hand and one at your left, in your glory." (Mark 10:35-37)

Seconds later, Jesus responds:

...but whoever wishes to become great among you must be your servant, and whoever wishes to be first among you must be slave of all. (Mark 10:43-44)

We have just heard a reading that speaks of power: power we might seek, power we might crave, power that can control. But the reading also speaks of power not just in terms of human power, but of God's power: power that serves, power that is shared, power that gives life. James, John, and the rest of the disciples find themselves caught wrestling in the dance of human power and God's power.

One day I was walking through my kitchen, and as I passed the sink, I saw an ant. Not even half a second went by before I found myself extending my forefinger, and having it meet the tile with the little ant in between. Squash! I continued my walk.

For whatever reason, I found myself reflecting on the ease with which I had killed the ant. Why was it so easy to squish the ant? Why didn't I feel awful about destroying part of God's creation? "What a dumb little ant," I thought. Of course, the reason I felt no remorse was because I am considerably larger than the ant—I compared my size to the size of the ant. The ant was insignificant to me. Power. I saw one more ant. Squash!

A voice continued to haunt me.

And then something new entered my mind. "Even though the difference between you and the ant is fairly large, it is nothing compared to the difference between you and God. And God is not going around finding sandwich material between forefinger and ground. Instead, God is extending a hand, extending a hand out to us, and inviting us to stand in the presence of God."

...and above all in the Word made flesh, Jesus, your Son. For in these last days you sent him to be incarnate from the Virgin Mary, to be the Savior and Redeemer of the world. In him, you have delivered us from evil, and made us worthy to stand before you. (Eucharistic Prayer B, *The Book of Common Prayer*)

James and John, the sons of Zebedee, came forward to him and said to him, "Teacher, we want you to do for us whatever we ask of you." And he said to them, "What is it you want me to do for you?" And they said to him, "Grant us to sit, one at your right hand and one at your left, in your glory." (Mark 10:35-37)

A request for power. Seconds later, Jesus responds:

...but whoever wishes to become great among you must be your servant, and whoever wishes to be first among you must be slave of all. (Mark 10:43-44)

Many children today, even our own children, are caught in a prison created by adults' desire for human power. Release comes only when adults around them have a change of desire for God's power—power that serves, power that is shared, power that gives life.

In our churches, release might look like allowing children the ability to *see* everything going on without finding their sight lines blocked by backs of pews or backs of others. Release could look like finding structures in Christian Formation which not only pass on the wisdom of the elders, but also provide equal avenues for the prophetic voice of the child to be shared with the adults. Do the adults hold claim to the right and left sides of the throne, or is the invitation for all to gather? Can we imagine children laying on hands and praying for those in need? Can we imagine children accompanying our Lay Eucharistic Visitors sharing holy gifts from the holy table? Will we listen to our children? Power that serves, power that is shared, power that gives life...

In our community, release might look like seeing that a child may live with a healthy mind, body, and spirit. Medical care, opportunities for good schools, and opportunities for work help provide a solid future on which hopes and dreams are nurtured. Release will look and feel safe—safe from guns, safe from drugs, safe from predators, safe from an environment that kills dreams and imagination. Will we give our children voice? Will we allow our children hope? Will we open every possible door to the grace of God's love? Will we untangle ourselves and others from the conflict between human power and God's power?

In Jesus there is freedom. In Jesus there is release. In Jesus there is life.

James and John, the sons of Zebedee, came forward to him and said to him, "Teacher, we want you to do for us whatever we ask of you." And he said to them, "What is it you want me to do for you?" And they said to him, "Grant us to sit, one at your right hand and one at your left, in your glory." (Mark 10:35-37)

A request for power. Seconds later, Jesus responds:

...but whoever wishes to become great among you must be your servant, and whoever wishes to be first among you must be slave of all. (Mark 10:43-44)

"THE BEST SEAT IN THE HOUSE"
Sample Children's Sermon
(based on Mark 10:35-45)

Where do you think is the best place to sit here in the church? Do you think it is there, in the pews? How about here on the steps [or wherever the children are gathered]? Do you think the best place to sit is up there by the minister? Does someone want to go try out that seat? [Allow one volunteer to try your seat.] Did that feel like a very special place to sit?

Guess what: I think that the best place may not even be here in this room! I think it is where the teacher is down in the nursery with the babies. Do you know why? Because Jesus said that getting the "best seat" isn't about being close up to the minister or someone who seems important. Jesus said the "best seat" is about being someplace where you can help other people. And the teacher in the nursery is helping children.

Now, most of you can't be a teacher in the nursery just yet, but there are lots of other places where you can help other children. And wherever you are helping other children is a great place to be. It may be on the playground, helping someone who fell and hurt herself. It may be in the lunchroom, when you sit with someone who is all by himself. It may be when you help a friend decide to tell the truth. It may be in your neighborhood when you make a new friend. Any place you are is the best place to be if you are helping another child.

Let's say a prayer:

Dear God,
Thank you for sending Jesus to be our helper.
Help us to help other children,
especially those who are hurt, hungry, lonely, or sad.
Amen.

"YOUR SONS AND YOUR DAUGHTERS SHALL PROPHESY": A MODEL FOR HELPING YOUTHS PREPARE FOR PREACHING

1. Gather a group of youths and distribute copies of the biblical readings that will be used on the Children's Sabbath. Ask them to read and pray the readings each day and open themselves to the day's events.

Ask them to consider the following:

A. How is the voice of God through the readings related to what I see or experience throughout the day?

B. What is God saying to me through the readings?

C. What memories are triggered from my own life experience or my knowledge of others' life experiences as a result of reading and praying the passages of scripture?

Let the group know that they will be sharing their insights at the next meeting.

2. At the next gathering, ask the youths to share their insights with one another. When all have had an opportunity to share, invite the group to do the following:

A. Name common threads or themes.

B. Call out particular stories or illustrations which were powerful.

C. Create an outline for a sermon/homily

Adults in the group may wish to exercise the gift of wisdom by sharing any particular revelations they had while listening to the youths.

3. The group may wish to ask one, two, or three persons to take responsibility for continuing the work and putting together the presentation. This work should occur before the next meeting.

4. At the final gathering, a presentation of the sermon/homily is made. The youths who are listening should be asked to share their observations.

A. What worked well in the presentation?

B. What message might be said with more conviction or clarity?

5. Those who are preaching should practice in the church to familiarize themselves with any equipment and practice pacing, eye contact, and projection.

(Prepared by the Rev. Ernesto R. Medina, Missioner for Christian Education, Episcopal Diocese of Los Angeles)

Daily Devotional Guide

No congregation rightly ministers to children without prayer as the source and sustenance of their ministry. Offer the following daily devotionals as a spiritual discipline to your congregation's members, to help them direct their hearts, minds, and prayer on children and the Children's Sabbath. Distribute the devotionals on the Sunday before the Children's Sabbath.

The devotions may be used at other times, as well. The readings, reflection, and prayer may strengthen youth group leaders preparing for a retreat, church school teachers at the beginning of a year, volunteers in a congregational program serving children and families, and others.

To create the devotional booklets: The "Christian Daily Devotional" pages are formatted horizontally to include two devotions per 8½" x 11" page. Make two-sided photocopies of the following pages in the order in which they are found. Fold each set of pages down the middle to create a 5½" x 8½" eight-page booklet. The cover page should begin "Christian Daily Devotional Guide" and the back cover should begin "Sunday, October 22." Staple the booklet in the fold, if desired.

Children's Activity Bulletin

The activity bulletin is designed for young children who will be in the sanctuary during the service of worship. Be sure to provide crayons or other appropriate writing instruments for the children to use in completing the bulletins.

To create the children's bulletin: Photocopy this insert on both sides of 8½" x 11" paper. Fold in the middle so that "Children's Activity Bulletin" appears at the top of the front page and "Stop! Look! Listen!" appears on the back.

CHRISTIAN DAILY DEVOTIONAL GUIDE

Joining Hearts, Hands, and Voices to Leave No Child Behind

October 16-22, 2000

by Shannon Daley-Harris

Sunday, October 22

Teaching Our Children: A Moral Start

"Teach them to your children, talking about them when you are at home and when you are away, when you lie down and when you rise." (Deuteronomy 11:19)

Giving our children a moral start isn't something that can be left up to others, such as church school teachers or pastors, and it isn't something that can be relegated to Sunday morning. As our passage today reminds us, imparting our understanding of God's will for and word to us isn't a task specific to time or place, it is a way of living.

Every place we find ourselves, whether at the breakfast table, in the car running errands, in line at the grocery store, or walking to the park, represents an opportunity to teach our children about what matters in life. Every time of day, from early morning mumbles over cereal bowls to the last sleepy snuggles before bed, offers moments to share what we value and to recall God's love.

What we teach our children in these times and places is, of course, much more than the sum of our words. It is how we live our lives, how we treat other people. We teach when we speak up on behalf of others, and by our silence before injustice. We teach when we extend care to children not our own, and when our prayers include children in need we may never meet. Again, teaching our children is not a task, it is a way of living. Let us live our lives in that knowledge.

Gracious God, you have taught us to love you and each other. Help me to live by your teaching, so that I may teach children—not just my own, but all whom I encounter and all on whose behalf I may speak out. Amen.

Monday, October 16

Children's Sabbath

So God blessed the seventh day and hallowed it, because on it God rested from all the work that he had done in creation. (Genesis 2:3)

"The Son of Man is lord of the sabbath." (Luke 6:5)

Although Sabbath is a word and concept with deep biblical roots in the Old and New Testaments, it still is strange to many of us.

Throughout scripture, we see different facets of the Sabbath. As our Genesis passage reminds us, the Sabbath is a holy time marking God's resting from the good work of creation. Sabbath, and the Children's Sabbath, may be for us a time of rest and renewal. Let the celebration lift your heart, rejuvenate your commitment, refresh your appreciation of children made in God's image.

The Sabbath is also a time to bring about restorative justice. The Sabbatical year, every seventh year, was a time when economic injustice and oppression were overturned, when right relationship and the chance for sufficiency were restored to all persons. The Children's Sabbath is a time to work for justice for all children, to speak out against the poverty, lack of health care, violence, failing schools, and other sources of oppression that deny our children full life.

When Jesus defied tradition and healed on the Sabbath, he reminded us that the Sabbath is a day, like every day, that we are called to serve and be healers. When the disciples plucked some food to eat on the Sabbath, Jesus reminded us that feeding the hungry is a priority even on the Sabbath. On the Children's Sabbath, find a way to reach out and meet an immediate hurt and need of a child. It may be the need for food or the hunger to be heard, a boost up to the water fountain or a thirst for learning. May your experience of this Sabbath be blessed and holy.

Creator God, you have made us in your image and charged us to be stewards of your creation. Help me to fulfill that charge by caring for others, especially the children, and seeking justice for those who are oppressed. Amen.

Saturday, October 21

Pray for the Peace of Jerusalem: A Safe Start for Every Child

Pray for the peace of Jerusalem: "May they prosper who love you. Peace be within your walls, and security within your towers." For the sake of my relatives and friends I will say, "Peace be within you." For the sake of the house of the Lord our God, I will seek your good. (Psalm 122:6-9)

This pilgrim's prayer was on my lips when I lived in Belfast, Northern Ireland, and taught children who lived in that violence-scarred community. There, children decorated a "Happy Birthday" poster for a classmate with pictures of tanks and guns—the landscape of their childhood.

This prayer is on my lips today, living in Washington, D.C., where children plan their funerals, stray bullets strike down seven-year-olds, a gun buy-back program reveals the extent of the arsenal loose in my community, and Congress in the Capitol building just blocks away fails to pass measures to keep children safe from these deadly weapons.

This prayer is on my lips when I learn that nearly 12 children are killed by guns and 218 children are arrested for violent crimes in our nation each day. When I read about Paducah and Jonesboro and Columbine. When I realize that violence is robbing children of their security, and no one is safe.

For the sake of our children, our families, and our friends, we must join in praying for peace—and living our prayers in action. Pray for the peace of Jerusalem and Jonesboro, of Columbine and our capital, pray for your community and our nation. For the sake of our children, our families, our friends, our congregations.

Gracious God, I pray for peace this day. I pray for those who do violence, and those who suffer violence. Bring your healing to the hearts of those who fear and those who are feared, those who are anxious and those who are angry, those who despair and those who destroy. Give me your peace, I pray, that I may draw upon it to work for peace in my community and in our nation. Amen.

Thursday, October 19

Surrounding Children with Nurture and Protection

But I have calmed and weaned my soul, like a weaned child with its mother; my soul is like the weaned child that is with me. O Israel, hope in the Lord from this time on and forevermore. (Psalm 131:2-3)

What a tender psalm this is, imparting such an aura of comfort and calm. It reminds me of my nighttime ritual with my young son.

Every night since my son's birth, as he nurses before sleep I have murmured into his cloud-soft hair, "Mommy loves Micah. Daddy loves Micah. God loves Micah. We will always love you." The time will come all too soon when he no longer nurses before sleep. But he will never be too old to hear those words of comfort and promise.

Now, of course, his limited vocabulary means we cannot "explain" God to him. We can only hope that he understands the link between the steadfast, joyous, constant love he experiences from his parents and the love of God we speak of in the same breath.

All children need to be surrounded by those who nurture and protect them. Parents, child care providers, teachers, congregation members, neighbors—all may help build up children's trust and assurance that they are loved and safe. When we extend such love and care to children, when their trust is preserved, they may come to learn of and believe in God's love and trustworthiness.

Tender God, thank you for your constant love for me, your child. Help me to express your love for children so that they may come to trust that they are loved by you. Amen.

Wednesday, October 18

Still Working for a Healthy Start

Jesus said to [the sick person], "Stand up, take your mat and walk." At once the man was made well, and he took up his mat and began to walk. Now that day was a sabbath. (John 5:8-9)

Jesus' healing a sick person on the Sabbath upset the religious authorities of the day. Tradition called for the cessation of all work and only rest on the Sabbath. This Sabbath rest would mirror God's rest on the seventh day after creating the world.

When the religious authorities discovered that Jesus had healed the man on the Sabbath, they challenged Jesus. *"But Jesus answered them, 'My Father is still working, and I also am working.'"* (John 5:17) Jesus' calling God his parent only further outraged the religious leaders.

Jesus' action and words here convey two important messages. First, God's creative action in our world is not something in the past. God did not leave humankind to its own devices after creating the world and then resting on the seventh day. Rather, Jesus affirms that God is *still* working in our world, working for our healing and wholeness. So, too, he and we are called to do God's work. This work is an ongoing process that invites our active participation.

Second, Jesus' actions and words also remind us that we are not to be limited or bound by tradition or convention or convenience or schedules when faced with human suffering and need. Religious tradition and rituals are important, but responding to the urgent needs of one who suffers is even more important.

Let our actions be fueled by this understanding today when, in our nation, 798 babies will be born at low birthweight, 406 babies will be born to women who had late or no prenatal care, and 1,540 babies will be born without health insurance. God is still working; let us work, too, to care for God's children.

Creating God, I thank you for your active presence in my life, working for healing and wholeness. Help me to join you in this work, offering comfort to children who suffer in mind, body, or spirit. This I ask in the name of the one who brought healing wherever and whenever people were hurting. Amen.

Tuesday, October 17

Leading At the Pace of Children: Leave No Child Behind

"I will lead on slowly...according to the pace of the children." (Genesis 33:14)

With these words, Jacob declines Esau's invitation to travel together. To do so would have meant driving the animals too hard and exhausting the children. As a result, some would have been unable to keep up, and would have been left behind.

Today, millions of children are being left behind while the world races on ahead of them. 13.5 million are left in poverty, while the economy zooms upward in the nation's biggest-ever economic expansion. 11.9 million are left without health insurance, while health technology and scientific discoveries advance with new breakthroughs. Thousands of children lag a year or more behind in school, while the job market requires increasingly complex skills and advanced degrees. Children are locked in jails or buried too young while violence overtakes them. Children are left to figure out their own values while the hectic pace of weekend schedules crowds out church attendance and family dinners.

To go at the pace of children means committing to leave no child behind. It means ensuring that all children have their basic needs met. That all children can get health care for preventive and sick care. That positive early learning experiences at home, in child care, and in preschool programs like Head Start prepare children to succeed in school. It means keeping our children safe at home, in school, and in the community. And it means taking time to worship with children, to pray and play with them, to walk and talk together—not just our "own" children, but other children, too. This week, and every week, let us go according to the pace of the children.

Gracious God, help me to take time out of my busy week to slow down and listen to you, and to children. Help me to see from their perspective, walk at their pace, and then help me to do what I should to see that no child is left behind. Amen.

Friday, October 20

Bringing the Good News: A Fair Start

The Spirit of the Lord is upon me, because he has anointed me to bring good news to the poor. He has sent me to proclaim release to the captives and recovery of sight to the blind, to let the oppressed go free, to proclaim the year of the Lord's favor. (Luke 4:18-19)

It began when two young sisters and their cousin knocked on the church door, and the pastor invited them to return the next day to tour the church and make cookies. Over time, their story unfolded—of life in a house overrun by drugs and strangers, of poverty that brought hunger and hopelessness. The good news the church offered came through counseling and friendship, support for the children's educational achievement, and ensuring that they were clothed and fed. It included the exciting day the children witnessed a baptism and wanted to be "bap-a-tized" themselves, continued through study of baptism's meaning, and culminated in a baptism that washed the children in baptismal water and the congregation in tears. The congregation continues to bring good news today as members guide and support the now-teenagers in the various challenges they face, and the pastor leads a community organizing effort to reduce violence and poverty and improve the local schools.

In our nation today, 13.5 million children live in poverty. Almost one out of every five. Very simply, that means that each of us can touch the life of a child who is poor. Each of us may prayerfully ask ourselves, how can I bring good news to a poor child? Invite a low-income family to church, or offer to bring children whose parents must work on the weekends. Donate books, clothes, food, toothbrushes, or "child-proofing" safety devices to be distributed to poor families. Volunteer in a program that serves poor children. Call upon your legislators to make just policies that are good news to poor children and their families. Pray.

Liberating God, I pray that your spirit will move through me that I may bring the good news to children in need. Help me to be a friend to those who are poor, left out, or looked down upon, just like Jesus was. Inspire me to be a voice for justice and the end of oppression, just like Jesus and the prophets before him. Amen.

Children's Activity Bulletin

Today is Children's Sabbath, a special day to say thank you to God for children and to promise to do our best to take care of children, especially those who need our help.

Draw a picture of yourself in the space below.

Dear God,
Thank you for me and for all children!

Stop!

Today is a good day to pay attention, and to keep your eyes and ears open, because church is going to be different! *Put a check if you notice that some of these things are different today.*

☐ Decorations in church like balloons or children's pictures
☐ Children being special helpers in church (like reading something or handing out programs)
☐ More children in church than last week

What else seems different? _____

Look!
During church today, look for these things. Put a check when you see them.

☐ A grown-up helping a child (taking their coat off, for example)
☐ A child helping another child
☐ Someone smiling at you
☐ Someone collecting money so the church can help children and other people who need it

What else do you see? _____

Listen!
During church today, listen for these things. Put a check when you hear them.

☐ A song about God
☐ A song about how God wants us to help other people
☐ A prayer that talks about children
☐ A child singing or talking

What else do you hear? _____

National Observance of Children's Sabbaths 2000

DEAR LORD, BE GOOD TO ME THE SEA IS SO WIDE AND MY BOAT IS SO SMALL

Children's Defense Fund

Jesus wants us to help children. Look for the hidden words on this list that tell about helping.

(If you don't know what a word means, ask a grown-up after church!)
Hint: words can go across, up and down and diagonally.

Words about children who need help:

hurt
lonely
hungry
sad
scared

Words about how we can help:

help	welcome
serve	feed
pray	cheer up
share	comfort
heal	

```
H U R T A W B P R A Y C
E D C E F E S A D G H I
L L O N E L Y D H E A L
P J M K L C M N A O P F
Q R F S H O T S E R V E
U V O W U M Z H Y Z E E
A B R C N E D A E F G D
H I T J G K L R M A N O
P Q R L Y C H E E R U P
```

Jesus helped children who were sick, hungry, left out, and sad. He told grown-ups that taking care of children is so important, it is like taking care of Jesus himself!

Draw a square around the picture of Jesus helping children. Draw a circle around each picture of someone else helping children. (If you want, you can color in the pictures.)

Christian Lesson Plans

The following Christian Lesson Plans are designed for a one-hour class. They may be used instead of your regular curriculum on the Children's Sabbath, incorporated into your curriculum, or used during a special Children's Sabbath educational session on the Children's Sabbath weekend or on a weekend or weeknight preceding the Children's Sabbath.

Several of the lesson plans have activities with end products that can be shared with the whole congregation, such as a mural or a dramatic presentation. Decide in advance how and when these results might be shared with the church. Will you present them after the education hour or after worship on the day of your Children's Sabbath? Will you extend the focus on children in need and share the created end products the following week? Or you may want to use these lessons the week before the Children's Sabbath so that, for example, the dramatic presentation could be incorporated into the Children's Sabbath service.

Please note: Whenever you raise problems facing children, there is the possibility that your own students are facing some of these concerns themselves. This calls for two kinds of preparation. First, you want to be sensitive to the students so they don't feel embarrassed or ashamed if you are talking about a problem that they are facing themselves. Second, you need to be prepared to respond to disclosures that may be prompted by the discussion, such as a conversation about children who are being hurt by a grown-up. Know in advance how you would respond to a disclosure and what resources you would turn to, such as the pastor or a child welfare hotline. Contact a director of an early childhood program or after-school ministry, a scout leader, or the local office of child welfare for information on how to get help in your community. Please don't let this caution deter you from raising these topics; just be prepared. You may end up making more of a difference in the life of a child than you could have imagined.

Lesson Plan for Preschool Children (ages 3-4)

Theme
"We Are Helpers"

Scriptural Passage
Mark 10:35-45

Focus
Helping others is the way to be special. Jesus helped people who were sick, poor, scared, left out, and learning to do the right thing. Jesus wants us to be helpers too. We can help other children who are hurt, hungry, scared, left out, or confused.

Lesson Objectives

The students will:
* Think about ways they are helpers.
* Learn about Jesus as a helper and as someone who wants us to be helpers.
* Identify adults who help children.
* Think about children who need help and ways they can help them.

Materials
* Noise-makers, such as maracas, tambourines, or a tape player and cassette tape of music
* Snack, napkins, and cups
* Mural paper and crayons or markers
* Magazines, scissors, glue, and stiff paper to prepare the pictures for the activity "Grown-Ups Who Help" (See Preparation below.)
* Baby doll, doll clothes, bottle, stroller, and other baby care items

Preparation
* Review page 55.
* Review the lesson.
* Assemble the materials.
* Make pictures for the activity "Grown-Ups Who Help." Cut out magazine pictures that show adults such as doctors, nurses, teachers, parents, and babysitters. Ideally, the pictures will show them caring for children. Parenting magazines may be good sources for such pictures. Glue or staple the pictures onto stiff paper.
* If you will be enacting the Bible story, recruit two others and practice it a few times.
* Write the heading "Jesus helped children, and so can we!" on the mural paper.

Overview

1. Introduce the Theme and Bible Message (Discussion, Bible Story) (10 minutes)

2. Explore the Message (Game, Discussion, Snack, Activities) (45-50 minutes)

3. Closing (5 minutes)

1. Introduce the Theme and Bible Message
Gather the children in a circle on the floor. Sit on the floor with them, or in a chair if you prefer.

Opening Discussion: What Are Ways You Are a Helper? (5 minutes)
Say, "Today we are going to talk about being helpers, and how we can help other children."

Ask the following questions, allowing time for the children to respond to each: "What are ways that you are a helper? Do you help clean up your toys? Set the table? Take care of a pet? Do you help get yourself dressed? Do you have a little brother or sister that you help take care of?"

Bible Story: It Is Good to Be a Helper! (5 minutes)
(You may want to prepare the following as a dramatic enactment with two other adults or youths. One portrays Jesus and two are his friends. The two friends should sit in the circle alongside the children. At the appointed time, they should push their way close to Jesus and say their lines.)

Say, "Once upon a time, Jesus was sitting together with his friends, just like we are sitting together here. Then, two of the friends pushed their way to Jesus. 'Hey, Jesus, we want to be very important and special. We want the best seats. We want to sit next to you. Will you promise us that we can be extra-special and have the best seats next to you?'

"Jesus said, 'The way to be important and extra-special is to help other people. I don't try to be most important but to help others.'

"Jesus was a good helper, and he wanted his friends to be good helpers, too. Jesus helped children and grown-ups who were sick and hurt, and made them feel better. Jesus helped people by caring about them and loving them. He helped people who were hungry get some food to eat. Jesus helped people be loving and not hate. And Jesus helped people learn how to do the right thing."

(If you are enacting this with two others, at this time have them show that they understand Jesus' message, and return to where they were originally sitting. Perhaps one of them can even offer to help the other one stand up, to reinforce the helping message.)

2. Explore the Message

Game: Jesus' Helpers (5 minutes)
Tell the children that they will be playing a game called Jesus' Helpers. In the game, an adult will be Jesus. The two children sitting next to Jesus in each round become Jesus' "helpers." To become helpers they must give up their special seats next to Jesus. Tell them that they are going to help by making music for the game. Their job is to make noise (by clapping their hands, shaking maracas or tambourines you have provided, or playing a tape). Like the game musical chairs, while they are making noise, the other children should stand and walk around the circle (while Jesus remains seated). When the noise stops, everyone should sit down. The two children who wind up sitting on either side of Jesus become the next "helpers" to make noise (and the previous helpers rejoin the game). Reinforce the message each round by saying to the helpers, "Thank you for giving up your special seat next to me so that you can be our helpers," or "Thank you for being such good helpers. It is an important job."

Discussion: Children Need Different Kinds of Help (5 minutes)
After the game, have the children be seated again for the following discussion.

Say, "Everyone needs to be helped in some way, at some time. Mommies need help. Daddies need help. Teachers need help."

"Some children face extra hard problems that need our help."

"Some children are sick or hurt, and need to visit a doctor. If you have been to a doctor, raise your hand. Isn't it good to have someone to help us get better?"

"Some children need a safe place to be while their parents are working. Who takes care of you during the day? *(Allow children to respond. Answers may include parents, grandparents, babysitters, child care teachers.)* Doesn't it feel good to have people to take good care of you and help you learn and have fun?"

"Some children don't have enough food to eat or warm clothes to wear or a place to live. How does it feel to be hungry? *(Allow time for responses.)* It's not a very good feeling, is it? Everyone is hungry some time, but some children are hungry a lot of the time because their parents don't have enough money to buy food."

Discussion: How Could You Help? (5 minutes)
Say, "Let's think of ways that we can help other children who need our help." Then ask the following questions, allowing the children time to respond to each.

- How could you help someone who fell down on the playground and was crying?
- How could you help someone who was hungry and didn't have any lunch to eat?
- How could you help someone who was cold and didn't have any mittens or a coat?
- How could you help someone who didn't know whether to lie or tell the truth? Who wanted to take something that didn't belong to them?

Snack (10 minutes)
Say, "Instead of the teacher giving each of you a snack, you can help each other get a snack. We are going to pass around a plate of *(whatever snack you have, such as cookies)*. Instead of taking one for yourself, take one and give it to the person next to you." Demonstrate how this works with the first child, prompting and guiding others as necessary. You may also want to have the children be helpers by setting out paper cups and napkins. At the end of the snack, encourage the children to be good helpers by cleaning up the napkin and cup of the person next to them.

Creative Activity: Jesus Helped Children, and We Can Help, Too! (10 minutes)
Have the children draw on a long piece of mural paper with the heading "Jesus helped children, and so can we!" Encourage the children to draw pictures of themselves helping another child. As drawings by children this age are likely to be a little "abstract," have them tell you about their pictures and add captions. Arrange to hang the mural in the church building where congregation members can see it.

Activity: Grown-Ups Who Help (5 minutes)
For this activity, hold up the prepared pictures and, for each, ask the children how this person is a helper and how they help children. Be open to a range of responses. First, hold up a picture of a nurse or a doctor. Next, hold up a picture of a teacher, parent, or babysitter. Next, a picture of someone who helps those who are poor or hungry. Next, show a picture of a police officer. Finally, show a picture of a minister or church school teacher.

Alternative: Lay the pictures on a table or on the floor or hang on a bulletin board. Ask the children to help you identify people who are helpers. There may be more than one right answer.

- Who helps children when they are sick?
- Who helps children learn at school or day care?
- Who takes care of children at home?
- Who helps children when someone hurts them?
- Who helps children when they are hungry?
- Who helps children learn about God?

Note: If time permits, you may want to bring in dress-up items and let the children pretend to be one of these kinds of helpers. You (and a team teacher, if you have one) could pretend to be a child in need of help, or you could pretend that the doll to be used in the next activity needs help.

Activity: Taking Care of the Baby (10 minutes)
Have a baby doll, blanket, diaper, clothes, bottle, and toy stroller. Ask, "who can help me put on the baby's diaper?" Pick a child who volunteers, and work together to put on the diaper. Affirm the child, noting, "You are a great helper. Putting on a diaper is an important job. You can help take care of other children. " Next, ask for a volunteer to help you put on the baby's socks, and so forth. Continue until each child has had an opportunity to help take care of the baby doll in some way.

3. Closing

Ask the children to be helpers right now, by putting away the crayons from the coloring activity, and putting the prepared pictures in an envelope or pile.

Have them come back to a closing circle and repeat each line of the following prayer after you.
Dear God *(children repeat, Dear God)*,
Thank you for sending Jesus
to be our helper.
Help us to be good helpers, too.
Amen.

Lesson Plan for the Elementary Grades

(with adaptations for grades K-2 and grades 3-5)

Theme
"Helping Others"

Scriptural Passage
Mark 10:35-45

Focus
Helping others is the way to be great. Jesus showed us how to help people who are sick, poor, scared, left out, and learning to do the right thing.

Lesson Objectives

The students will:
- Learn about Jesus as someone who helped others and wants us to be helpers.
- Learn about children in need and reflect on ways that they can help other children.
- Participate in an active response to help children in need.

Materials
- Index cards
- Large bowl
- Snack food, beverage, cups, and napkins
- Please see activity options in *Respond to the Message*, and gather the materials noted in the activity or activities you select.

Preparation
- Review page 55.
- Read through the lesson and gather the materials required.
- Practice telling the story. If you will be acting it out, recruit two others and practice.
- Familiarize yourself with the material in the discussion in *Explore the Message*. Alternatively, find pictures for each of the sections (for example, a child who is hurt, a child who looks scared, a child with a caregiver). Parenting magazines may be good sources for such pictures. Cut the pictures out, and paste each one on a separate piece of paper. On the back of the paper, write the information and questions provided for each section. During the discussion you can hold up the picture for the children to see, while you can refresh your memory for the discussion by reading what you have written on the back.

- Write the grab bag questions (one for each student) on index cards and put in the bowl. (Don't write out the "start" headings, which are simply provided to help you see the range of topics addressed.) Make up additional questions if needed.
- Please see activity options in *Respond to the Message*, and conduct any preparation noted in the activity or activities you select.

Overview

1. Introduce the Theme and Bible Message (5 minutes)
2. Explore the Message (Discussion, Grab Bag Questions, Snack, Game) (35 minutes)
3. Respond to the Message (15 minutes)
4. Closing (1-5 minutes)

1. Introduce the Theme and Bible Message

Say, "Today is Children's Sabbath, a special day when our church looks for ways that we can help other children, such as children who are sick, or hungry, or scared, or don't have someone to take care of them when their parents are at work."

Say, "In class today, we are going to talk about being helpers, just like Jesus was a helper, and do a project to help other children. To begin, let's learn a story about Jesus and his friends."

(Option: Present the Bible story as a dramatic enactment. With three others, either adapt the passage below to have a narrator, Jesus, and two friends, or use the script on page 70.)

Say, "Once upon a time, Jesus was sitting together with his friends, just like we are sitting together here. Then, two of the friends pushed their way to Jesus. 'Hey Jesus, we want to be very important and special. We want the best seats. We want to sit next to you. Will you promise us that we can be extra-special and have the best seats next to you?'

"Jesus said, 'The way to be important and extra-special is to help other people. I don't try to be most important but to help others.'

"Jesus was a good helper, and he wanted his friends to be good helpers too. Jesus helped children and grown-ups who were sick and hurt, and made them feel better.

Jesus helped people by caring about them and loving them. He helped people who were hungry get some food to eat. Jesus helped people be loving and not hate. And Jesus helped people learn how to do the right thing."

(If you are enacting this with two others, at this time have the friends show that they understand Jesus' message, and return to where they were originally sitting. Perhaps one of them can even offer to help the other one stand up, to reinforce the helping message.)

2. Explore the Message

Discussion: Children Who Need Our Help

(5 minutes)

YOUNGER ELEMENTARY VERSION:

Ask, "Who needs to be helped in some way, at some time?" *(Accept the answers they come up with. Add mothers, fathers, teachers, ministers, and children, if the children do not offer these answers.)*

Say, "Some children face extra hard problems that need our help."

Continue, "Some children are sick or hurt, and need to visit a doctor. Raise your hand if you have ever been to the doctor." *(Allow time for a show of hands.)* "When children are sick or hurt, it is important to have someone who can help them get better. Children need a Healthy Start."

Say, "Some children need a safe place to be while their parents are working. Who takes care of you after school?" *(Allow children to respond. Answers may include parents, grandparents, babysitters.)* "Doesn't it feel good to have people to take good care of you? Children need the Head Start of good, loving care."

Say, "Some children don't have enough food to eat or warm clothes to wear or a place to live. How does it feel to be hungry?" *(Allow time for responses.)* "It's not a very good feeling, is it? Everyone is hungry some time, but some children are hungry a lot of the time because their parents don't have enough money to buy food. It's not fair that some children are hungry; all children need a Fair Start."

Say, "Some children are scared because they don't feel safe. They are worried about being hurt by someone. Have you ever been scared? What are some of the things that help you feel safe?" *(Answers may include a parent or adult, a toy, a pet, a friend.)* "All children need a Safe Start."

Ask, "Who are some of the people who help you know the difference between what is right and what is wrong, and help you do the right thing? Who are some of the people who help you learn about God?" *(If children need further*

guidance, you may want to ask them about any of the following: parents, older brothers and sisters, teachers, church school teachers, and the minister.) Say, "It is important to have people who help us learn to do the right thing. All children need a Moral Start."

Conclude, "There are lots of people who can help children. There are parents and grandparents and doctors and teachers and school nurses and police officers and ministers and babysitters and more. You know who else can help children? You can!"

OLDER ELEMENTARY VERSION:

With older students, you may want to have a more open-ended discussion than the guided discussion above. If so, use the opening questions noted below, and then tailor your responses based on what the children come up with. If students provide openings, try to underscore the five major areas of children's health, child care, poverty, violence, and the need for moral guidance/learning to do the right thing.

Ask, "Who needs to be helped in some way, at some time?" *(Accept the answers they come up with. Add mothers, fathers, teachers, ministers, and children, if the children do not offer these answers.)*

Say, "Some children face extra hard problems that need our help. What hard problems do some children have?"

Depending on their answers, use responses like these:

"When children are really sick or hurt, it is important to be able to see a doctor to help them get better. It's also important to be able to see a doctor for check-ups to help children can stay healthy. All children need a Healthy Start."

"When children need a safe place to be, it feels good to have people take care of them, like parents or babysitters. Children need a Head Start of good, loving care."

"When children don't have enough food to eat (or warm clothes to wear or a place to live), they need help. It's not fair that some children are hungry most of the time, or don't have a place to live. All children need a Fair Start."

"When children are scared because they don't feel safe or because they are being hurt, they need someone to help them feel safe. All children need a Safe Start."

"When children don't know whether to lie or tell the truth, they need friends and parents who can encourage them to do the right thing. All children need a Moral Start."

"When children are worried they won't do well on a test, and are tempted to cheat, they need friends and family who tell them that it is more important to be honest and do the right thing than to get a high grade on a test. All children need a Moral Start."

Grab Bag Questions: How Could You Help?
(10 minutes)

Have the children take turns picking an index card out of the bowl and answering the question. (Provide assistance reading the question, as needed, with younger children.) Once the child who picked the question has responded, other children may volunteer additional ideas. Remind the children that there are some situations that children can't handle by themselves, and the best way to help then is by getting an adult to help, too.

Grab Bag Questions

Children need a Healthy Start:
- How could you help someone who hurt herself on the playground during recess?
- How could you help someone who is sick but whose parents don't have money to take him to the doctor?
- How could you help someone who is having trouble seeing the chalkboard but hasn't told anyone?

Children need a Head Start:
- How could you help someone who is scared to stay home alone after school, but doesn't have anywhere to go?
- How could you help someone who doesn't have anyone to help her with her homework?

Children need a Fair Start:
- How could you help someone who is hungry and doesn't have any lunch?
- How could you help someone who doesn't have a warm winter coat and whose parents don't have money to buy one?
- How could you help someone who is being teased about not having a telephone or computer at her house because her parents don't have the money?
- How could you help someone who is being teased about not having the "cool" kind of sneakers because he couldn't afford them?

Children need a Safe Start:
- How could you help someone who is being hurt by a grown-up?

- How could you help someone who is scared to walk home because her neighborhood is dangerous and has a lot of fighting?
- How could you help someone who is angry at someone else?
- How could you help someone who was told he'll be beaten up after school?
- How could you help someone who wants to show you the gun her parents own?

Children need a Moral Start:
- How could you help someone who told a lie because he is worried about getting into trouble?
- How could you help someone who has a question about God?
- How could you help someone who wants to steal something from a store?
- How could you help someone who wants to do something you know is wrong?

Affirm the students' responses as they are offered, with comments like "You would be a great helper if you did that," or "I think that's just the kind of help Jesus wants us to give people." If a student proposes an inappropriate idea, you might say, "I can tell you really care about trying to help someone who has a problem," and, as needed, offer assistance redirecting the solution.

Snack (10 minutes)

Take a break for snack time. Encourage the children to help each other, by passing napkins and the snack foods. Affirm their helping behavior.

Game: Helping Each Other (10 minutes)

Pair the children up (designating one in each pair as "A" and the other as "B"). Have them line up on one side of the room, and indicate the "finish line" on the other side of the room. (You may choose to go outside or to another place in the church if there is not enough space in your classroom.) For the first round, tell the children that they must cross the room, but the A's cannot use one foot, and the B's must close their eyes. The children in each pair must help each other to cross the room. Affirm even the last pair to cross the line, saying, "Remember, Jesus taught us that being first is not the most important thing; helping each other is." For the second round, tell the A's that they must walk backwards (with B's keeping them from walking into other children), and the B's must hop on one foot (holding on to A's for balance). Again, affirm that the process of helping each other was more important than who crossed the line first. Make up a few more rounds, if time and interest permit.

3. Respond to the Message

Select one of the following projects (or several, if you want to set up activity centers):

- **Have the children decorate brown paper bags that will be filled with items to be distributed at a food pantry serving families.** Have them use materials such as crayons, markers, pictures cut from magazines, and stickers. While they are working, talk with them about children who are hungry, and how those children will feel when the bag is filled with good food to eat. *Optional:* Ask each child to bring in a non-perishable food item (such as peanut butter, baked beans, or ravioli in a can) the next week to put in the bags. If there is extra time, have the children make friendly cards to tuck into each bag. An alternative would be to fill the bags with baby care items, such as diapers, diaper wipes, baby food, baby shampoo and soap.

- **Have the children make "Feel Better" cards for children in the hospital.** Contact the pediatric wing of a local hospital in advance, and get the names of children who would appreciate receiving cards. Give each child an 8½" x 11" piece of paper folded in half and then in half again to form a blank card. Guide the students in writing appropriate messages inside, and then have them decorate the front and back with crayons, markers, or stickers. While they are working, talk with them about children who are hurt and sick. Note that some children can't even see a doctor when they are sick because their parents don't have enough money. Affirm that your students are being good helpers like Jesus, and that some sick children will feel better when they receive the cards. (If there is extra time, the children could make drawings to decorate a waiting room of your community's health clinic.)

- **Have the children come up with a "Peacemaker Plan" that lists steps to reduce violence and keep children safe.** Have younger children dictate their plans to you to write down on posterboard; older children can write their out themselves. Both groups can illustrate the poster. Suggest scenarios and have them come up with several ideas for each: "If you are feeling angry at someone you can help by..." "If you see two children having a fight you can help by..." "If you are someplace where there is a gun (at school, at a friend's house, etc.) you can help by..." "If someone you know is being hurt by a grown-up, you can help by..."

4. Closing

Gather the children in a circle for your closing time. Ask the children to think about a time when someone helped them. Tell them you are going to begin the prayer and will give them a chance to add their own. Begin by saying, "Thank you, God, for sending Jesus to be our helper and to teach us how to help other people. Thank you for people who have helped us. Thank you for (add your own example)." Then, invite the children to add their own "thank you's" to God for a time they were helped. End the prayer by saying, "Help us to remember that being great isn't about being first, it is about helping other people. Amen."

Lesson Plan for Middle School (Grades 6, 7, & 8)

Theme
"Put Yourself in Their Shoes"

Scriptural Passage
Mark 10:35-45

Focus
Service is the way to be great. Jesus showed us how to help people who are sick, poor, scared, left out, and learning to do the right thing.

Lesson Objectives

The students will:
- Learn about Jesus as someone who served others and wants us to serve others.
- Learn about children who need our help today.
- Reflect on ways that they can be great by serving other children.
- Participate in an active response to help children in need.

Materials
- Index cards, pencils
- Flip chart paper and markers (optional)
- Copies of page 70, "Who Is the Greatest?"
- Please see activity options in *Respond to the Message*, and gather the materials noted in the activity or activities you select.

Preparation
- Review page 55.
- Familiarize yourself with the lesson plan.
- Make copies of "Who Is the Greatest?," one per student.
- Please see activity options in *Respond to the Message*, and conduct the preparation noted in the activity or activities you select.

Overview

1. Introduce the Theme and Bible Message (Thought Tickler, Opening Discussion, Read the Bible Story, Discussion) (25 minutes)
2. Children Need to Be Great By Helping Them (Activity: Put Yourself In Their Shoes) (15 minutes)
3. Respond to the Message (20 minutes)
4. Closing (1 minute)

1. Introduce the Theme and Bible Message

Thought Tickler
As the students arrive, give each one an index card and pencil. Ask each student to list five things that make someone great or a leader—what qualities do they have, how do they act?

Opening Discussion
Remind the students that today is Children's Sabbath, a day when churches and synagogues all across the country are learning more about problems facing children and youths and committing to help them. Tell them that in today's class you will be talking about what it means to be "great" and a leader, and how they can be great leaders that help children in need.

Invite the students to share the ideas they came up with in the opening "Thought Tickler" exercise. Then invite the students to discuss the following questions. (You may want to record ideas on flip chart paper headed "Being First...Being Last.")

How does a person get to be first in something? How do you get to be first in a class, in athletics, in a job, financially, in popularity?

What is good about being first like that?

What happens to the people who are last in these situations? How do they feel? How are they treated? (Be prepared to redirect inappropriate responses that "put down" people who are "last." Add that in a minute they will be hearing about how Jesus feels about people who are last.)

Read the Bible Story and Discussion
Hand out copies of "Who Is the Greatest?," based on Mark 10:35-45. Invite students to read different parts. (Alternatively, distribute "Who Is the Greatest?" and invite students to read it to themselves.)

Introduce it by saying, "What did Jesus say to his friends about what it really means to be first and greatest? Let's see." Afterward, discuss the questions at the bottom of the page.

2. Children Need Us to Be Great by Helping Them
Introduce the next section by saying, "We've talked about how Jesus wants his followers to be great by helping other people, especially those who are 'last.' We've had some important ideas about how things might be different in school or our community if we understood being great as

serving others. Now, we are going to talk about children who really need us to help them, children who are being left behind, and then we will take some action to help children have a Healthy Start, a Head Start, a Fair Start, a Safe Start, and a Moral Start in life."

Activity: Put Yourself in Their Shoes

Have the students line up. Outline a circle in another part of the room, either by using children's shoes which you have brought in (or asked the students to bring in) or by putting down masking tape. Tell the students, "We are going to learn about some of the problems facing children across our nation by 'putting ourselves in their shoes.' I am going to ask questions about some statistics (or 'numbers'). When I tell you the statistic, like 'one out of every four,' let's have every fourth person move into the circle."

Then, using the statistics in "Put Yourself In Their Shoes," have the students separate themselves accordingly. For example, say, "Do you know how many preschoolers have a mother who works, and need someone else to take care of them, like a relative, child care center, or babysitter?" Say, "One out of every two preschoolers needs some kind of child care." Then, every other student (i.e., one in two) should move into the designated circle. Encourage them to figure out how to group themselves accurately, but guide them if necessary. Then, ask the students to get back into a line. Say, "Do you know how many children will be poor at some point in their childhood?" Say, "One out of every three children will be poor at some point in their childhood." Then every third student should move into the circle. Continue with the rest of the statistics.

At the end of the exercise, ask the students to share their reactions. Which statistics surprised them the most? What do they think about the problems described? What do they think they should do? What do they think the church, community, or government should do?

3. Respond to the Message

Select one or more activities below for your class to do.

Serve Children by Raising Awareness

• Have the students make a collage to be displayed in the church building to raise awareness of the adults. Suggest a heading such as "Put Yourself In Their Shoes." Have the students do the following: Trace around their shoes on construction paper and cut out the footprints. In the center of each, write a different fact from the previous exercise. Paste the footprints on the mural paper, and add additional illustrations, thoughts, prayers, poems, or pictures of children from magazines.

• Have the students practice a dramatic presentation of the *Put Yourself In Their Shoes* activity above to present to the congregation, perhaps during the coffee hour or social time following the worship service. (If you plan to do this the same day, be sure to make the appropriate arrangements in advance.)

Serve Children by Speaking Out

• Have each student write a letter to one of their legislators that describes the problems they have learned about, urges solutions, and asks for a reply. Give them copies of the sample format in Section 6. Be sure to have on hand paper, envelopes, stamps, and the names and addresses of legislators.

Serve Children by Reaching Out

• Have the students participate in a service activity to help children. For example, have them plan a shoe drive to collect children's shoes and winter boots (new or in good condition) to donate to an organization serving children in need. Have them decorate a collection box to be placed in the church building to collect donations of baby care items or food to be distributed to families in need. Or, have the children assemble first aid kits (with adhesive bandages, antiseptic ointment, syrup of ipecac, infant or children's pain reliever, baby thermometer, and other items you have purchased) to be donated to families that need them. See Section 6 for more ideas.

4. Closing

Gather the students and close with this prayer or one of your own.

"Dear God, we thank you that in sending Jesus you put yourself into our shoes. We know that you understand our hurts, needs, and hopes in a personal way. Help us to put ourselves in the shoes of others, especially children in need, so that we may know their hurts, needs, and hopes. Then, we pray, help us to respond faithfully to serve them. Amen."

PUT YOURSELF IN THEIR SHOES

Children need and deserve a Healthy Start:
- 1 in 6 children has no health insurance.
- 1 in 6 babies is born to a mother who had no prenatal care during the first three months of pregnancy.

Children need and deserve a Head Start:
- 1 in 2 preschoolers has a mother in the labor force.
- 1 in 3 students is a year or more behind in school.
- 1 in 8 students never graduates from high school.

Children need and deserve a Fair Start:
- 1 in 3 children will be poor at some point in childhood.
- 1 in 5 children is poor right now.
- 1 in 5 children lives in a family receiving food stamps.
- 1 in 7 children lives with a working relative but is poor nonetheless.

Children need and deserve a Safe Start:
- Every day, 6 children commit suicide in our nation.
- Every day, 10 children are homicide victims.
- Every day, 12 children are killed by guns.

(Data from *The State of America's Children 2000* by the Children's Defense Fund.)

Lesson Plan for High School (Grades 9-12)

Theme
"Who Is the Greatest?"

Scriptural Passage
Mark 10:35-45

Focus
Service is a way to be great. Jesus showed us how to help people who are sick, poor, scared, left out, and learning to do the right thing.

Lesson Objectives

The students will:
- Learn about Jesus as someone who served others and wants us to serve others.
- Learn about children who need our help today.
- Reflect on ways that they can be great by serving other children.
- Participate in an active response to help children in need.

Materials
- Copies of "Being Great," and pencils or pens
- Copies of "Who is the Greatest?"
- Index cards
- Large bowl
- Please see activity options in *Respond to the Message,* and gather the materials noted in the activity or activities you select.
- Optional: microphone on a microphone stand

Preparation
- Review page 55.
- Make copies of "Being Great," one per student.
- Make copies of "Who Is the Greatest?," one per student.
- Write each of the facts in "Sound Bite Facts" on a separate index card and place in the large bowl. (Don't write out the "start" headings; they are simply to help you see the areas covered.)
- Please see activity options in *Respond to the Message,* and conduct the preparation noted in the activity or activities you select.

Overview

1. Introduce the Theme and Bible Message (Thought Tickler, Introduction, Bible Message, Discussion) (15 minutes)
2. Explore the Message (Sound Bites) (25 minutes)
3. Respond to the Message (Activity Options) (20 minutes)
4. Closing (Litany) (1 minute)

1. Introduce the Theme and Bible Message
Thought Tickler
As students arrive, give them the handout "Being Great." Ask them to read the quote by the Rev. Dr. Martin Luther King, Jr.. Ask them to write their own definition of what makes someone great.

Introduction
Remind the students that this weekend is Children's Sabbath, when congregations across the nation are focusing their worship services, education programs, and activities on learning more about children's needs and ways we can respond in prayer, service, and advocacy.

Tell them that in today's lesson they will be learning about what Jesus told his followers about serving others and being great, and then putting the lesson into action to help children who are being left behind. Together, you will work to give children a Healthy Start, a Head Start, a Fair Start, a Safe Start, and a Moral Start in life.

Bible Message and Discussion
Ask for volunteers to share their definitions of greatness from the "Thought Tickler" exercise. Tell them that they will be doing a dramatic reading to hear Jesus' definition of greatness.

Ask for volunteers to read the dramatic reading "Who Is the Greatest?" Afterward, discuss the questions listed at the bottom of that page.

2. Explore the Message
Introduce the next section by saying, "We've talked about what it means to be great, and how Jesus wants us to be great by serving others. Now we are going to look at some children who have serious needs and ways that we can be great by helping them. Today, too many children are being left behind. Every child needs a Healthy Start, a Head Start, a Fair Start, a Safe Start, and a Moral Start."

Activity: Sound Bites

Ask the students to define a "sound bite." (A "sound bite" is a short sentence or two that really catches your attention because it tells you something important or surprising in an interesting way that you are likely to remember.)

Give them one or more of the following examples. (Before class starts, you may want to invite another teacher or students who have arrived early to prepare to read the following examples as if they were radio or TV spots.) "Nearly 12 children are killed by guns each day. That is the equivalent of a classroom full of children dying from guns every two days. Let's learn something really important: we've got to work together to stop the violence." "Nearly 1 in 5 children is poor in our nation. While we sit down to dinner tables loaded with good food tonight, one out of every five children in our country may not be sitting down to any dinner at all, or one so small that they still go to bed hungry." "You know how your stomach growls and aches a little sometimes in the class period right before lunch? It sure feels great to get to lunch, doesn't it? Imagine if your stomach felt that hunger all the time, if you never got enough to eat. Well, the nearly 1 in 5 children who are poor in our nation don't just imagine it; they live it every day. Let's do something about it."

Have each student choose an index card from the bowl. If the class is large, have them work in pairs or repeat some of the facts. Give them five minutes to write a "sound bite" about the fact on their index card, as they would hear in a radio or TV spot. (Encourage them to let you know if they don't fully understand their fact.) Remind them that they want to catch our attention and make us remember their fact. (Tips: comparing a number to something familiar; contrasting circumstances to highlight differences; using vivid, emotional words.)

Sound Bite Facts

Children need a Healthy Start:
11.9 million children don't have health insurance (1 in every 6 children).

Children need a Head Start:
13 million children are in child care, including 6 million babies and toddlers.
1 in 2 preschoolers has a mother who works. 2/3 of mothers of young children work outside the home, many out of economic necessity.

Children need a Fair Start:
13.5 million children are poor (nearly 1 in 5 children).

Children need a Safe Start and a Moral Start:
Nearly 12 children are killed by guns each day.
218 children are arrested for violent crimes each day (one every 7 minutes).
5,044 children are arrested each day.

After the students have written their sound bites, have them take turns reading them aloud. If you want, you can play a "news anchor" to set it up. (If available, use a microphone on a stand to enhance this activity.) Say, "This is your anchor [make up a goofy name or use your own], bringing you an important story on the status of children from our reporters in the field. Take it away, [name of the first student to read]."

Invite the students to react to what they learned in the sound bites. Which facts surprised them? How do these facts make them feel? Angry? Hopeless? Determined? Sad?

Encourage them to memorize their sound bite and share it with others in the coming week to help raise awareness about children's problems. Emphasize that sound bites can be helpful in calling attention to the problems, but that action is needed to make a difference.

3. Respond to the Message

Emphasize that we can help solve the problems described in the sound bites. We can serve children in need by raising awareness about the problems, by reaching out to them, and by speaking up on their behalf.
Select one or more of the following activities for your class to do as a whole or in smaller groups.

Serve Children by Raising Awareness

- Have the students make a collage to be displayed in the church building to raise awareness. Have them come up with a heading, such as "The Way to Greatness Is by Serving Children in Need: Leave No Child Behind." Have them write their sound bites on mural paper and add drawings or pictures cut from magazines featuring children, parents, and those who help children such as teachers and doctors; prayers; poems; and other thoughts.

- Have them practice the "news report" (perhaps with a student playing the "anchor" this time) to present to the congregation, possibly during the coffee hour or social time following the worship service. Alternatively, use a video camera to tape their newscast to show to the congregation or other church school classes. If you will be presenting this to the congregation on the same day as the lesson, be sure to make appropriate arrangements in advance.

Serve Children by Reaching Out

- Have the students focus on one of the five "starts": a Healthy Start (health), a Head Start (early childhood nurture and education), a Fair Start (child poverty), a Safe Start (safety), or a Moral Start (moral grounding). Next, have them brainstorm the different sources of support or organizations that are meeting the need. For example, a Fair Start (child poverty) might be addressed by the welfare office, a church food pantry, a community soup kitchen, Habitat for Humanity, the agency which distributes housing subsidies, and job training programs. Then, have them brainstorm the kinds of volunteer support and donations they think could be useful. For example, donations could include food, clothing (children's clothes and adult's job interview clothing), books and toys, diapers, and baby items like high chairs and safety gates. Volunteer help might include distributing food at the pantry, playing with children at the welfare office while parents are in line, and building a Habitat house. Encourage them to think about gifts and skills that they have that could be unique contributions. Finally, help students decide if they would like to pursue one of these possibilities. You may want to research some organizations before-

hand to determine if help is needed. The students could spearhead a collection drive in the congregation to gather the donation items or sign up to volunteer as a group or individually on successive weeks.

Serve Children by Speaking Out

- Have each student write a letter to one of their legislators that describes the problems they have learned about, urges solutions, and asks for a reply. They can use their sound bites in the letters. Give them copies of the sample format in Section 6. Be sure to have on hand paper, envelopes, pens, stamps, and the names and addresses of legislators.

- Have them write a similar letter to the editor of your local paper. This could be done as a group letter or individually. They may want to refer to the Children's Sabbath.

4. Closing

Gather the students and tell them that you will conclude with a "litany," a prayer that alternates lines between a leader and the rest of the people. Ask the students to read their sound bites again, and after each student reads, have the whole class respond by saying, "Lord, help us to lead by serving children."

"BEING GREAT"

"Everybody can be great, because anyone can serve. You don't have to have a college degree to serve. You don't have to make your subject and your verb agree to serve. You don't have to know about Plato and Aristotle to serve. You don't have to know Einstein's theory of relativity to serve. You don't have to know the second theory of thermodynamics in physics to serve. You only need a heart full of grace. A soul generated by love." (Dr. Martin Luther King, Jr.)

What I think makes someone great:

WHO IS THE GREATEST?

(Based on Mark 10:35-45, Good News translation)

James & John: *(speaking together, to Jesus)* Teacher, there is something we want you to do for us.

Jesus: What do you want me to do for you?

James: When you sit on your throne in the glorious Kingdom, we want you to let us sit with you...

John: ...one at your right and one at your left.

Jesus: You don't know what you are asking for. Can you drink the cup that I must drink? Can you be baptized in the way I must be baptized?

James & John: *(speaking together)* We can.

Jesus: *(sadly and thoughtfully)* You will indeed drink the cup I must drink and be baptized in the way I must be baptized.

But I do not have the right to choose who will sit at my right and my left. It is God who will give these places to those for whom God has prepared them.

Other disciples: *(nudge each other, grumble, call out to James and John)* "Apple-polisher!" "Trying to be the teacher's pet, huh?" "Serves you right, trying to get to him before we do!" "You always want to be first in everything."

Jesus: *(gestures to them to come towards him)* You know that those who are considered rulers over the people have power over them, and the leaders rule over them. *(Disciples all nod.)* This, however, is not the way it is among you. *(Disciples start to look puzzled.)* If one of you wants to be great, you must be the servant of the rest; and if one of you wants to be first, you must be the slave of all. For even I did not come to be served; I came to serve and to give my life to redeem many people.

Discussion Questions:

- What do you think Jesus meant when he talked about the cup he must drink and his baptism? What was he trying to warn or prepare the disciples for? What kinds of difficulties can people experience when they are trying to do what God wants?

- Why do you think the other disciples were upset with James and John? Do you think it is because they thought James and John were wrong to make the request, or were the other disciples mad that they hadn't gotten to ask Jesus first?

- What do you think the main point of this reading was? How would you put the main message in your own words?

- How would you put the last part Jesus said into a modern situation? That is, what would he be saying about our school, church, or community?

- Imagine...How would things be different if we turned things upside down, like Jesus did, and understood greatness as serving others? How could school be different? How could athletics be different? What about popularity with other kids—how would that be different? How would the "in" crowd act? What about money—how we earn it, save it, and spend it? How would our families, church, and community be different?

Lesson Plan for Adults

Theme
"Putting the Last First"

Scriptural Passages
Mark 9:33-37, Mark 10:35-45

Focus
Jesus taught that greatness comes not from power and privilege but from serving others and by putting those who are last, especially children, first.

Lesson Objectives

Participants will:
- Explore scriptural passages and their implications for serving children in need.
- Learn more about the needs of children today.
- Consider ways they can serve children and help to put them first.

Materials
- Bible
- Flip chart paper and markers
- Copies of handouts on pages 73-74 and 75
- Pens and pencils

Preparation
- Review the lesson plan.
- Make a copy of the handouts for each participant.

Overview

1. Opening and Introduction to the Message (15 minutes)
2. Explore the Message (10 minutes)
3. Respond to the Message (30 minutes)
4. Closing (5 minutes)

1. Opening and Introduction to the Message
Welcome participants to the class. Remind them that this weekend is the Children's Sabbath, a time when congregations of many faiths across the nation are uniting in a focus on children in need.

Say that today, children are being left behind, are last, or are at the bottom of the heap in many ways. Today's scriptural passages offer Jesus' perspective on the reversals of power and privilege that true and faithful service requires. Together, the class will consider what it would mean to put Jesus' message into action for children today.

Ask for a volunteer to read Mark 9:33-37. Ask for a second volunteer to read Mark 10:35-45.

Invite the class to respond to the following questions about the passages.

- What do you think was the main point of each passage? Are the main messages the same or are there differences? How would you put the main message of each passage in your own words?

- Given that all of the disciples were arguing about who was the greatest in the passage from Mark 9, why do you think that the disciples became angry with James's and John's request in Mark 10.41? Do you think they were upset about the inappropriate request or were the other disciples mad that they hadn't gotten to ask Jesus first?

- What do you think Jesus meant when he talked about the cup he must drink and his baptism? What was he trying to warn or prepare the disciples for? What kinds of difficulties have you experienced when you have sought to serve God? How do such difficulties affect our willingness to serve children and others in need?

2. Explore the Message
Tell the class that in the passage from Mark 9, Jesus' taking a child in his arms and relating serving the child to serving him and God was revolutionary. It can be hard to appreciate how shocking his words were, because today we often idealize children and regard our own children (at the very least) as treasures to be protected and loved. But children in Jesus' day were essentially "non-persons," and could not have been further removed in status from the male, adult disciples of a famous teacher. To urge the disciples to welcome the children, and to find greatness in serving them, was radical.

Who Is Being Left Behind?
Tell the class that even though we usually don't regard our own children as "last" or utterly without privilege or status, there are many children today whose circumstances make them "last" or "least," like the child Jesus put among his disciples.

Ask the class to compile a list of the children who are being left behind and are "last" today. (For example, "children who are homeless," "children who have been abandoned by both parents.") Record their ideas on flip chart paper.

Distribute copies of the handout "Children Today Are Being Left Behind." Have class members take turns reading paragraphs aloud.

Provide time for people to share their reactions or responses when the reading is complete, especially in light of the scriptural passages that were discussed earlier.

3. Respond to the Message

How Can We Put Children First?
What Do They Need?

Tell the class that although there are countless children being left behind today, the good news is that we can work together faithfully to serve children and give them the start in life that they need and deserve.

Distribute copies of the handout "Leave No Child Behind." Divide the group into five small groups, if your class is large enough. (Otherwise, divide into fewer small groups or keep the class together and do the brainstorming as one large group.) Assign one of the "starts" to each of the small groups. Ask them to brainstorm ideas for how individuals, congregations, communities, and the nation can help every child have that start. Have them record their ideas on flip chart paper. After 10 minutes, reconvene the group and have each small group report on their ideas.

Decide if there are one or more ideas that the group would like to put into action.

Campaigning for the Children: Looking for Servant-Leaders to Put Children First

Remind participants that this is an election year. While it is inappropriate (and illegal!) for congregations to engage in partisan politics (working for or against a particular candidate or political party), it is entirely appropriate for congregations and members to consider what concerns their faith calls them to stand up for, and what kind of leadership embodies the principles of justice and compassion.

Ask each participant to think about what a candidate for political office ought to stand for that would put children first. If a legislator is serious about public *service*, what commitments should we expect them to make for children's well-being?

Ask each participant to write five priorities political leaders should have in order to truly put children first. When they are done writing, invite them to share their priorities aloud. This should not be seen as a time for debate. Each person's priorities, like the vote she or he casts, are a personal decision for them to make, hopefully illumined by the information presented and discussion they have engaged in.

4. Closing

Tell the class that in the closing prayer, you will begin and then encourage them to add their own prayers silently or aloud. Tell them the first part will be a time to pray for children being left behind. Ask them to conclude each petition with "Lord in your mercy," to which the whole group will respond, "Bless the children." Tell them that the second part of the prayer will be a time to pray for those who could help children. Ask them to conclude each of these petitions with "Lord in your mercy," to which the group will respond, "Help them to serve." (It may be helpful to write out the two responses on flip chart paper to help people remember.)

Leader: Loving God,
We pray this day for the children who are being left behind...
For the children who are victims of violence, Lord in your mercy,

Group: **Bless the children.**

[Allow time for individuals to add petitions for other children who are left behind.]

Leader: We pray this day for all who have the potential to give children the start they need...
For the legislators and other elected officials, Lord in your mercy,

Group: **Help them to serve.**

[Allow time for individuals to add petitions for others who could help children.]

Leader: We ask these things in the name of the one whose arms embraced children and who patiently helped his friends to know you. Amen.

CHILDREN TODAY ARE BEING LEFT BEHIND

(All of the following stories are true. The names marked by an asterisk have been changed to protect the privacy of those involved.)

Children Need a Healthy Start

When Bobby*, a preschooler from a New England city, scratched a mosquito bite on his leg, the area became infected. His parents took him to a doctor, who prescribed an antibiotic. But because Bobby's father earned very low wages at his job, the family could not immediately afford to buy the prescription.

As a result of the family's poverty, the infection grew dangerously out of control, and Bobby was hospitalized for three days in order to receive intravenous antibiotics. Doctors estimated that each of those hospital days cost about $800.

Children Need a Head Start

Until recently, Bernadette Monteleone and Charles Lampkin's child care expenses were so high that they constantly worried about how to buy food or pay the rent on time. Preschool costs for both Charles Edward, 3, and Chelsea, 5, ran $100 a week. Together, the couple earns under $20,000 a year, not enough to afford such high child care payments. In February 1998, however, Bernadette received word that the state child care assistance she'd applied for months before came through. This help is now saving the family roughly $60 a week.

"Before we received the subsidy, it was very difficult, and a lot of times we came up short," Bernadette says. "It gives us a little extra money to put toward bills   rent, utilities, and bus passes—and to help buy food and clothes for the children."

Toby Simon, on the other hand, is one of the many parents in America who make too much to qualify for state assistance, but too little to afford full-time child care. Last September Toby, who earns $35,000 a year, made arrangements for her daughter Hattie, nearly 2, with a family child care provider. She explained that she doesn't have much money, and the provider agreed to give Toby a price break, charging her $200 a week instead of $275.

After a few months, though, the provider informed Toby that Hattie would have to leave. She was told that parents who could afford to pay full price for care were clamoring for space with the provider, who desperately needed the extra money. Now Toby is searching for an alternative arrangement that she can afford.

"Hattie had been really happy there, and I thought she was doing very well," says Toby. "I was just completely devastated by this."

The Monteleone-Lampkins and the Simons are just two of the millions of working families in the United States who are struggling to find and keep quality, affordable child care. Bernadette and Charles's story has a happy ending, but for parents like Toby and many others, there seems to be no relief in sight.

Children Need a Fair Start

Sally* and her husband have been separated from their children for more than three months because they cannot find a place to live. After they lost their apartment because they could not afford the rent increase, the family lived in their car until the weather turned cold. Then, in desperation, the father secretly sheltered his children during the night in the warehouse where he worked, stopping when he feared that he would lose his

(continued on page 74)

(continued from page 73)

job if discovered. Without a place to live, the parents finally put their children in the temporary care of the state welfare division, which placed them in separate foster homes. The children, still apart, are having increasing problems in school, and their parents have been unable to find an affordable apartment that will accept the whole family.

Children Need a Safe Start

"Hi. My name is Bakari Clay and I'm going to tell you all about my neighborhood. The neighborhood I live in wasn't bad until about a year ago. It used to be safe and clean until they started to sell drugs and do drive-bys and stick people up. I think that people are so dumb for killing each other over drugs, coats, shoes, chains, and other material items. Some days I'm scared to even walk to school by myself thinking I'm gonna get killed....

But I just take a deep breath and keep my head to the sky, hoping that the police or someone can make my neighborhood safe to live in again someday. There's trouble anywhere you go so I'm gonna do all I can to help my neighborhood be the cleanest and safest place I can but I'm only eight years old—I can't do it all by myself." (From *My Neighborhood: The Words and Pictures of Inner-City Children*, compilation and narrative by Linda Waldman, 1993, Hyde Park Bank Foundation, Chicago.)

Children Need a Moral Start

High school senior Miguel DeJesus of New Britain, Conn., had a lot going for him. He was enrolled in a college preparatory course. Both of his parents had jobs. He and his mother were involved in their Baptist church. But Miguel wrote this in a youth literary magazine about the children of his generation:

> "The innocence is gone. Never again will kids be able to go outside and not be exposed to drugs, hunger, or poverty. The youth of today have nothing to do. They have no place to go. Especially here in New Britain, it's dead out here. We don't even have a movie theater. Then you wonder why we have so many gangs out here. If you have nowhere to go and nothing to do you feel alone, and when you feel alone you need to belong to something. When we have nothing to do, some of us turn to drugs and alcohol. The end of innocence is here....The [kids] don't know the academics, but they know the streets, and they think that's all they need to know."

On November 8, 1993, three months after writing this, Miguel was shot and killed on the steps of his high school.

Unless otherwise noted, all stories were previously published in CDF Reports.

LEAVE NO CHILD BEHIND

No child should be left behind. Every child needs and deserves a Healthy Start, a Head Start, a Fair Start, a Safe Start, and a Moral Start in life.

A Healthy Start means that children have healthy bodies and minds, and are assured a comprehensive health and mental health system that provides preventive care when they are well and treatment when they are ill.

A Head Start means that children have strong parents from birth who are supported by communities that truly value families, get the early childhood foundation they need to get ready for school, and attend high quality schools that inspire, respect, and support every child's success.

A Fair Start means that children grow up in families with jobs that pay livable wages and are protected from poverty, hunger, and homelessness when parents cannot adequately provide.

A Safe Start means that children are safe and secure in their homes, neighborhoods, and schools, are protected from the guns that kill a child every two hours, and have safe havens before and after school and during summer months.

A Moral Start means that parents, other caring adults, and congregations recognize and communicate every child's sacred worth and guide children by example in developing positive, enduring values of justice, compassion, and respect for self and others. Children of all ages need loving limits, discipline, and attention to successfully navigate the paths to adulthood.

Jewish Shabbat and Education Resources

T his section provides suggestions for the services, passages relating to children from the Torah, Prophets, and Talmud, a service for Shabbat and weekdays, and a sample sermon. It also includes lesson plans for all ages. The following suggestions are derived from the Conservative, Reconstructionist, and Reform traditions. Draw from those which are appropriate for your congregation.

Suggestions for the Services

This year, the National Observance of Children's Shabbats falls on Simchat Torah. This confluence of events creates a special opportunity to tie together the Children's Shabbats with consecration. Please use these materials to enhance your congregation's Simchat Torah celebration, or save them for another Shabbat.

Services on the Children's Shabbat are an excellent opportunity to help focus the congregation on the links between Torah readings, Jewish tradition, and advocating for children. They also serve as a time to affirm the work of your congregation on behalf of children, and to challenge members to continue and expand their responses to the needs of children locally and nationally.

The following suggestions may assist you in planning your own unique Children's Shabbat service or supplementing your congregation's weekly prayer and discussions.

- **There are several options for the services: 1) Use or adapt the service provided here, 2) develop your own Children's Shabbat that reflects the theme of children and the need for action, or 3) use readings from the prayer books that include a social action theme.** (Reform congregations may want to select a service with social action themes from *Gates of Prayer*, such as service number 4.)

- **Determine ways in which the children of your congregation can participate in the various services on this Shabbat.** Involve children attending religious school, members of youth groups, and children who attend the day school. For example, religious school classes and youth groups could read prayers, Torah and Haftorah readings, lead songs or responsive readings, greet people as they arrive, or design and print the bulletin. Keep in mind, however, that this is a family event and should not be "given over" to the children as "performers."

- **Focus the sermon, D'var Torah, or Torah discussion on children.** Emphasize helping every child have a Healthy Start, a Head Start, a Fair Start, a Safe Start, and a Moral Start in life. (For a guide to additional sermon resources in this manual, please see page 40.)

- **Invite a professional from the congregation or the community who works with or on behalf of children to give the sermon.** This might be a health care professional, a child care or Head Start provider, or staff from an organization or agency serving low-income families, for example.

- **On Friday night, incorporate the parental blessing for children into the service.** Or incorporate the need to bless all children into the Shabbat morning blessing of Bar/Bat Mitzvah children.

- **Honor congregation members who are working to nurture and protect children.** Ask them to lead certain prayers or give them Aliyot during the Torah reading.

- **Collect tzedakah in religious school to benefit a program serving children** such as a community health clinic, Head Start program, tutoring program, shelter for homeless families, or after-school program.

- **Distribute or insert the bulletin inserts found in Section 2.**

- **With the help of your Cantor, prepare some new music** to be sung by the children at the service.

- **Encourage families to invite grandparents and other relatives to join them for the service.** If you wish, plan a special recognition of grandparents during the service.

- **Arrange for a special *kiddush/oneg Shabbat/ luncheon/s'udah shlishit* in honor of the occasion.** As a resource, see "Planning a Shabbat or Holiday Family Meal" and "A Family Shabbaton," both from the Youth/School Liaison Department of the Women's League for Conservative Judaism.

- **Continue the celebration of Children's Sabbath with a *M'laveh Malkah* on Saturday evening or at the Sunday morning *minyan*/Religious School sessions.**

Passages Related to Children from the Torah, Prophets, and Talmud

By the breath of children God sustains the world. (Talmud Bavli, Shabbat 119b)

When the children are blessed, the parents by this very token are blessed. (Zohar, i, 227b)

Healthy Start:

For behold! I am creating a new heaven and a new earth; the former things shall not be remembered, they shall never come to mind. Be glad then, and rejoice forever in what I am creating. For I shall rejoice in Jerusalem and delight in her people. Never again shall be heard there the sounds of weeping and wailing. No more shall there be an infant or a graybeard who does not live out his days. (Isaiah 65:17-20a)

For the hurt of my poor people I am hurt, I mourn, and dismay has taken hold of me. Is there no balm in Gilead? Is there no physician there? Why then has the health of my poor people not been restored? (Jeremiah 8:21-22)

Head Start:

Rabbi Hamnuna said: Jerusalem was destroyed only because the children did not attend school, and loitered in the streets. (Pesikta Rabbati 29b)

The guardians of a city are the teachers of the young and the instructors of the old....If you see cities uprooted, know that it came about because they did not maintain their teachers' salaries. (Hagiga 1:7)

Fair Start:

Take care of the children of the poor, for they will be the ones who advance knowledge. (Nedarim 81a)

Speak up for [those unable to speak], for the rights of all the unfortunate. Speak up, judge righteously, champion the poor and needy. (Proverbs 31:8-9)

Safe Start:

The work of righteousness shall be peace, and the result of righteousness shall be quietness and confidence forever. (Isaiah 32:17)

One violates Shabbat for the sake of a one-day-old baby, but not for the corpse of David, King of Israel. (Shabbat 15b)

My chosen ones shall outlive the work of their hands. They shall not toil to no purpose; They shall not bear children for terror, but they shall be a people blessed by the LORD, and their offspring shall remain with them. (Isaiah 65:22-23)

Moral Start:

One who teaches a child Torah is considered to have taught that child and that child's children and grandchildren, to the end of the generations. (Kuddushin 30a)

And Israel beheld Joseph's sons and said, "Whose are these?" And Joseph said to his father, "These are my children, whom the Lord has given to me in this place." And he said, "Bring them to me, and I will bless them." (Genesis 48:8-9)

A Service for Shabbat and Weekdays

Words of Our Mouths, Thoughts of Our Hearts

Friday, October 20, 2000

Margaret Lange
Director of Education
Temple B'nai Jehudah
Kansas City, Mo.

This service features the Central Conference of American Rabbis' Gates of Prayer for Young People, which speaks eloquently to the hearts and spirits of children. (Reprinted with permission from the CCAR.) Additional prayers and readings were created for this service by Miss Stacey Yukon's 3rd grade class at Temple B'nai Jehudah in Kansas City, Mo..

Opening

We have come together to share and to sing. Our words are prayers. Our prayers are about the most important things in our lives and the people we love. When we pray, we talk to God. Sometimes we say our prayers so that our friends can also hear them, and sometimes we listen carefully to ourselves.

This place, too, is special. When Jews gather together to pray, that place becomes holy. This place is holy.

Before we begin, we must be very quiet…and listen.
The air around us is filled with sound:

> Our breathing, in and out;
> The beating of our hearts;
> Many secret, little sounds.

But we only hear when we open our ears…and our minds… and our hearts. Maybe we even hear that God is with us. As we prepare to pray, be very still now. Concentrate. Listen.

WHISPERS

A CHILD'S LOVE IS LIKE A WHISPER,
GIVEN IN LITTLE WAYS WE DO NOT HEAR
BUT IF YOU LISTEN CLOSELY IT WILL BE VERY CLEAR.

THEY OFTEN DO NOT SAY IT LOUD BUT IN HOW
THEY COME TO YOU…
DADDY, WILL YOU PLAY WITH ME?
MOMMY, TIE MY SHOE?

…THE MANY WAYS THEY TELL YOU CHANGES AS
THEY GROW
DAD, I MADE THE TEAM TODAY!
MOM, I'VE GOT TO GO!

DAD, I'VE GOT SOMETHING TO TELL YOU…I THINK
SHE IS THE ONE.
MOM, HE ASKED ME TO MARRY HIM. WOULD YOU
LOVE HIM AS YOUR SON?

A CHILD'S LOVE IS LIKE A WHISPER,
GIVEN IN LITTLE WAYS WE DO NOT HEAR
BUT IF YOU LISTEN CLOSELY IT WILL BE VERY CLEAR.

IT IS NEVER ENDING
A BLESSING FROM ABOVE
LISTEN TO THE WHISPERS OF A CHILD'S LOVE.

by Megan Klugman

DEAR GOD,

THERE ARE CHILDREN ALL OVER THE WORLD THAT
NEED HELP BECAUSE THEY STARVE IN POOR LANDS.
SOME KIDS ARE KIDNAPPED OR HURT.

GOD PLEASE HELP US GIVE AID TO THE CHILDREN
WHO NEED IT AND HELP US TO STOP OTHER CHILDREN
FROM BEING HURT.

by Greer Gaddie

Sh'ma and Its Blessings

Please rise

Bar'chu et Adonai ham'vorach.

בָּרְכוּ אֶת יְיָ הַמְבֹרָךְ:

Baruch Adonai ham'vorach
l'olam va-ed

בָּרוּךְ יְיָ הַמְבֹרָךְ
לְעוֹלָם וָעֶד:

Creation

All things bright and beautiful;
All things great and small;
All things wise and wonderful—
Dear God, You made them all.

Each lovely flower that opens;
Each little bird that sings—
You made their glowing colors;
You made their tiny wings.

The purple peaks of mountains;
The rivers flowing by;
The sunsets and the morning
That brightens up the sky;

The cold wind in the winter;
The pleasant summer sun;
The ripe fruits of the garden—
You made them every one.

You gave us eyes to see them
And lips that we might tell
How great are You, Almighty,
Who make all things well.

DEAR GOD,

YOU LOVE THE LAND OF ISRAEL AND THE CITY OF
JERUSALEM. HELP US WORK FOR OUR JEWISH HOME-
LAND. HELP US GO TO SLEEP IN PEACE, O GOD, AND
TO WAKE UP IN THE MORNING. WE FEEL YOU WITH
US WHEN WE DO MITZVOTH.

by Sam Rapshutz

Revelation/Love

Ahavat olam
Beit Yisra-eil
am'cha ahavta.

אַהֲבַת עוֹלָם
בֵּית יִשְׂרָאֵל
עַמְּךָ אָהָבְתָּ.

Long ago the Jewish people discovered God's love.
They listened for God's word,
And wrote in the Torah what they heard:
Worship only God.
Don't make idols.
Don't break a promise.
Remember to celebrate Shabbat.
Honor your father and your mother.
Don't steal.
Don't be unfaithful to your husband or wife.
Don't murder.
Don't be jealous of what other people have.
Don't tell lies.
Thank You, God, for these words.
When we read them, we know how to live, and we
remember that you love us.

Baruch ata, Adonai,
oheiv amo Yisra-eil.

בָּרוּךְ אַתָּה יְיָ,
אוֹהֵב עַמּוֹ יִשְׂרָאֵל:

Sh'ma Yisra-eil:
Adonai Eloheinu,
Adonai echad!

שְׁמַע יִשְׂרָאֵל,
יְיָ אֱלֹהֵינוּ,
יְיָ אֶחָד:

Hear, O Israel: the Eternal One is our God,
the Eternal God alone.

Baruch Sheim k'vod malchuto
l'olam va-ed!

בָּרוּךְ שֵׁם כְּבוֹד מַלְכוּתוֹ
לְעוֹלָם וָעֶד.

Blessed is God's glory forever and ever!

Please be seated

V'ahavta et
Adonai Elohecha
b'chol l'vav'cha,
uv'chol nafsh'cha.
uv'chol m'odecha,
V'hayu had'varim
ha-eileh asher
anochi m'tzav'cha
hayom al l'vavecha.
V'shinantam l'vanecha
v'dibarta bam
b'shivt'cha b'veitecha,
uv'lecht'cha vaderech,
uv'shochb'cha
uv'kumecha.
Uk'shartam l'ot
al yadecha,
v'hayu l'totafot
bein einecha.

וְאָהַבְתָּ אֵת
יְיָ אֱלֹהֶיךָ,
בְּכָל-לְבָבְךָ,
וּבְכָל-נַפְשְׁךָ,
וּבְכָל-מְאֹדֶךָ.
וְהָיוּ הַדְּבָרִים
הָאֵלֶּה, אֲשֶׁר
אָנֹכִי מְצַוְּךָ
הַיּוֹם, עַל-לְבָבֶךָ:
וְשִׁנַּנְתָּם לְבָנֶיךָ,
וְדִבַּרְתָּ בָּם
בְּשִׁבְתְּךָ בְּבֵיתֶךָ,
וּבְלֶכְתְּךָ בַדֶּרֶךְ
וּבְשָׁכְבְּךָ,
וּבְקוּמֶךָ.
וּקְשַׁרְתָּם לְאוֹת
עַל-יָדֶךָ,
וְהָיוּ לְטֹטָפֹת
בֵּין עֵינֶיךָ,

Uch'tavtam al m'zuzot
beitecha uvish'arecha.
L'ma-an tizk'ru
va-asitem
et kol mitzvotai,
vih'yitem k'doshim
leiloheichem.
Ani Adonai
Eloheichem,
asher hotzeiti
etchem
me-Eretz Mitzrayim
lihyot lachem
leilohim.
Ani Adonai
Eloheichem.

וּכְתַבְתָּם עַל מְזֻזוֹת
בֵּיתֶךָ וּבִשְׁעָרֶיךָ:
לְמַעַן תִּזְכְּרוּ
וַעֲשִׂיתֶם
אֶת־כָּל־מִצְוֹתָי,
וִהְיִיתֶם קְדֹשִׁים
לֵאלֹהֵיכֶם:
אֲנִי יְיָ
אֱלֹהֵיכֶם,
אֲשֶׁר הוֹצֵאתִי
אֶתְכֶם
מֵאֶרֶץ מִצְרַיִם,
לִהְיוֹת לָכֶם
לֵאלֹהִים,
אֲנִי יְיָ
אֱלֹהֵיכֶם:

You shall love God in every way you can.
Treat the Torah with love and respect.
Teach the Torah to your children when you grow up.
Talk about the Torah at home and everywhere.
Say the Sh'ma when you lie down
and when you rise up.
Place a mezuzah on your doorpost.
Do what the words in the Torah say to do.
Think about the words in the Torah
wherever you are,
whatever you are doing.
Remember to follow the ways of Torah.
Try to be holy like God.

DEAR GOD,

CHILDREN FEEL SAFE WHEN ADULTS PROTECT THEM
AND KEEP THEM SAFE. THE ADULTS OF THE WORLD
SHOULD KEEP CHILDREN SAFE. CHILDREN SHOULD
BE SAFE.

by Julia Siegel and Morgan Mendal

Redemption

Long ago, the Jewish people were slaves in Egypt. You sent
Moses to help our ancestors, so they could go free to worship
You. They sang a song to thank You:

Mi chamocha
ba-eilim, Adonai?

מִי כָמֹכָה
בָּאֵלִים יְיָ,

Who is like You, God of the universe?

Still today there are people who are not free.
We pray that they will be set free.
Then all who worship You still sing for joy:

Mi chamocha
ba-eilim, Adonai?
Mi kamocha,
ne'dar bakodesh,
nora t'hilot,
osei feleh?
Malchut'cha
ra-u vanecha,
bokei-a yam
lifnei Mosheh.
Zeh Eli!
Anu v'am'ru:
Adonai yimloch
l'olam va-ed!

Baruch ata, Adonai,
ga-al Yisra-eil.

מִי כָמֹכָה
בָּאֵלִים יְיָ,
מִי כָמֹכָה
נֶאְדָּר בַּקֹּדֶשׁ,
נוֹרָא תְהִלֹּת,
עֹשֵׂה פֶלֶא:
מַלְכוּתְךָ
רָאוּ בָנֶיךָ,
בּוֹקֵעַ יָם
לִפְנֵי מֹשֶׁה,
זֶה אֵלִי
עָנוּ וְאָמְרוּ:
יְיָ יִמְלֹךְ
לְעוֹלָם וָעֶד.

בָּרוּךְ אַתָּה יְיָ,
גָּאַל יִשְׂרָאֵל:

We praise You, Eternal God.
You freed the Jewish people from slavery.

DEAR GOD,

STOP PEOPLE FROM FIGHTING. IF PEOPLE FIGHT WE
WILL DIE AND SOON BE EXTINCT. PEOPLE ONLY MAKE
SITUATIONS WORSE IF WE FIGHT. KIDS WILL BE REALLY
SAD IF THEIR DADS GO INTO WAR AND NEVER COME
BACK. PLEASE STOP THE WARS.

by Claire Ellingson

God's protection

Help us to go to sleep in peace, O God,
and to wake up in the morning feeling good.

Guard us from harm outside our houses and inside them.
Like a mother bird protects her young with her covering
wing, please protect us.

Baruch ata, Adonai,
shomeir amo
Yisra-eil la-ad.
We praise You, Eternal God.
You always guard. Your people Israel.

בָּרוּךְ אַתָּה, יי,
שׁוֹמֵר עַמּוֹ
יִשְׂרָאֵל לָעַד.

Dear God

LET THERE BE NO MORE KIDNAPPING OR BAD THINGS HAPPENING TO CHILDREN, FOR AS LONG AS THIS WORLD EXISTS. PLEASE GRANT THIS WISH THAT I WISH TODAY. CHILDREN HAVE A RIGHT TO LIVE IN A PEACEFUL WORLD.

by Gregory Jacobs

For Shabbat

V'sham'ru	וְשָׁמְרוּ
v'nei Yisra-eil	בְנֵי־יִשְׂרָאֵל
et ha-Shabbat,	אֶת־הַשַּׁבָּת,
la-asot et ha-Shabbat	לַעֲשׂוֹת אֶת־הַשַּׁבָּת
l'dorotam	לְדֹרֹתָם
b'rit olam.	בְּרִית עוֹלָם.
Bini uvein	בֵּינִי וּבֵין
b'nei Yisra-eil,	בְּנֵי יִשְׂרָאֵל,
ot hi l'olam.	אוֹת הִיא לְעֹלָם.
Ki sheishet yamim	כִּי שֵׁשֶׁת יָמִים
asa Adonai	עָשָׂה יהוה
et hashamayim	אֶת־הַשָּׁמַיִם
v'et haaretz,	וְאֶת־הָאָרֶץ,
uvayom hash'vi-i	וּבַיּוֹם הַשְּׁבִיעִי
shavat vayinafash.	שָׁבַת וַיִּנָּפַשׁ.

The children of Israel shall keep the Sabbath in every generation. It is a covenant for all time. For in six days God made the heavens and the earth. And on the seventh day God rested.

Please rise

T'filah

Baruch ata, Adonai,	בָּרוּךְ אַתָּה, יי,
Eloheinu veilohei	אֱלֹהֵינוּ וֵאלֹהֵי
avoteinu v'imoteinu:	אֲבוֹתֵינוּ וְאִמּוֹתֵינוּ:
Elohei Avraham,	אֱלֹהֵי אַבְרָהָם,
Elohei Yitzchak,	אֱלֹהֵי יִצְחָק,
veilohei Ya-akov.	וֵאלֹהֵי יַעֲקֹב.
Elohei Sara,	אֱלֹהֵי שָׂרָה,
Elohei Rivka,	אֱלֹהֵי רִבְקָה,
Elohei Lei-a,	אֱלֹהֵי לֵאָה,
veilohei Racheil.	וֵאלֹהֵי רָחֵל.
Ha-eil hagadol	הָאֵל הַגָּדוֹל
hagibor v'hanora,	הַגִּבּוֹר וְהַנּוֹרָא,
eil elyon,	אֵל עֶלְיוֹן,
gomeil	גּוֹמֵל
chasadim tovim	חֲסָדִים טוֹבִים
v'konei hakol,	וְקוֹנֵה הַכֹּל,
v'zocheir chasdei	וְזוֹכֵר חַסְדֵי
avot v'imahot,	אָבוֹת וְאִמָּהוֹת,
umeivi g'ula	וּמֵבִיא גְאֻלָּה
liv'nei v'neihem,	לִבְנֵי בְנֵיהֶם,
l'ma-an sh'mo	לְמַעַן שְׁמוֹ
b'ahava.	בְּאַהֲבָה.
Melech ozeir	מֶלֶךְ עוֹזֵר
umoshi-a umagein.	וּמוֹשִׁיעַ וּמָגֵן.
Baruch ata, Adonai,	בָּרוּךְ אַתָּה, יי,
magein Avraham	מָגֵן אַבְרָהָם
v'ezrat Sara.	וְעֶזְרַת שָׂרָה.

We praise You, We praise You,
Eternal God: Eternal God:
God of Abraham, God of Sarah,
God of Isaac, God of Rebekah,
God of Jacob, Leah and Rachel,
God of all generations.

You are powerful, God,
and You can do anything.

You help us feel safe when we are afraid,
and make us feel better when we are sick.

Blessed is our God,
Shield of Abraham and Sarah.

Blessed is our God,
Creator of Life.

God, everywhere we turn
we feel Your power and Your holiness.
We feel You with us
when we hear a newborn baby cry.

Kadosh, kadosh, kadosh.   קָדוֹשׁ, קָדוֹשׁ, קָדוֹשׁ.

We feel You with us when we touch a soft flower.

Holy, holy, holy.

We feel You with us when we see a rainbow after a storm.

Kadosh, kadosh, kadosh.   קָדוֹשׁ, קָדוֹשׁ, קָדוֹשׁ.

We feel You with us when we are loving and loved.

Holy, holy, holy.

We feel You with us when we do a mitzvah.

Kadosh, kadosh, kadosh.   קָדוֹשׁ, קָדוֹשׁ, קָדוֹשׁ.

Baruch ata, Adonai,	בָּרוּךְ אַתָּה יְיָ,
ha-El hakadosh.	הָאֵל הַקָּדוֹשׁ.

We praise You, Eternal God.
Everywhere we turn, You are there.

Please be seated

Precious Day (For Shabbat)

Thank you, God, for Shabbat.
It is an important day. It is a holy day.

On Shabbat we remember You created the world.
On Shabbat we remember to be holy.
On Shabbat we feel close to You.
On Shabbat we feel close to our family.
May our lives be blessed on this Shabbat and
every Shabbat.

Baruch ata,
Adonai, m'kadeish
ha-Shabbat.

בָּרוּךְ אַתָּה,
יי, מְקַדֵּשׁ
הַשַּׁבָּת.

We praise You, Eternal God. You make Shabbat holy.

Yism'chu
v'malchut'cha
shom'rei Shabbat
v'kor'ei oneg.
Am m'kad'shei
sh'vi-i, kulam
yisb'u v'yit-an'gu
mituvecha.
V'hash'vi-i
ratzita bo
v'kidashto.
Chemdat yamim
oto karata,
zeicher l'ma-asei
v'reishit.

יִשְׂמְחוּ
בְמַלְכוּתְךָ
שׁוֹמְרֵי שַׁבָּת
וְקוֹרְאֵי עֹנֶג.
עַם מְקַדְּשֵׁי
שְׁבִיעִי, כֻּלָּם
יִשְׂבְּעוּ וְיִתְעַנְּגוּ
מִטּוּבֶךָ.
וְהַשְּׁבִיעִי
רָצִיתָ בּוֹ
וְקִדַּשְׁתּוֹ.
חֶמְדַּת יָמִים
אוֹתוֹ קָרֵאתָ,
זֵכֶר לְמַעֲשֵׂה
בְרֵאשִׁית.

Prayers of Asking (For Weekdays)

We thank You, God, for minds that think.
And we pray to use them well.
We thank You for helping us do what is right.
And we pray to know right from wrong.
We thank You, God, for hands that heal.
And we pray that our bodies be strong.
We thank You for letting us talk with You.
And we pray that you will always hear our prayer.

Peace

We pray for peace.
Peace for everyone, everywhere.

Peace for soldiers fighting wars.
Peace for people who live where soldiers are fighting around them.

Peace for parents who are worried about their children.
Peace for children who are worried about their parents.

Peace for people who are struggling with others.
Peace for people who are struggling with themselves.

Sim shalom,
tova uv'racha.

שִׂים שָׁלוֹם,
טוֹבָה וּבְרָכָה.

— OR —

Shalom rav
al Yisra-eil
am'cha
tasim l'olam,
ki ata hu
melech adon
l'chol hashalom.

שָׁלוֹם רָב
עַל יִשְׂרָאֵל
עַמְּךָ
תָּשִׂים לְעוֹלָם,
כִּי אַתָּה הוּא
מֶלֶךְ אָדוֹן
לְכָל־הַשָּׁלוֹם.

V'tov b'einecha
l'vareich et
am'cha Yisra-eil
b'chol eit
uv'chol sha-a
bish'lomecha.

וְטוֹב בְּעֵינֶיךָ
לְבָרֵךְ אֶת־
עַמְּךָ יִשְׂרָאֵל
בְּכָל־עֵת
וּבְכָל־שָׁעָה
בִּשְׁלוֹמֶךָ.

Baruch ata, Adonai,
osei hashalom.

בָּרוּךְ אַתָּה, יי,
עוֹשֶׂה הַשָּׁלוֹם.

*We praise You, Eternal God. You help us make peace. And you help us
find peace.*

DEAR GOD,

WAR SHOULD STOP BECAUSE…PEOPLE GET INJURED
AND SOMETIMES KILLED. IT IS A TRAGEDY TO SEE
SUCH A THING, BECAUSE IT USUALLY IS ABOUT PEOPLE
WANTING LAND OR MATERIAL THINGS. AGAIN WAR IS
AN ACCIDENT WAITING TO HAPPEN. SOME KIDS ARE
FORTUNATE ENOUGH NOT TO BE INVOLVED IN WAR.
WE WOULD LIKE TO HELP OTHERS. GOD WILL HELP
AND WILL BE WITH US ALWAYS.

by Gabrielle Choikhit

A Prayer of Responsibility for Children

We pray for children who put chocolate fingers everywhere, who like to be tickled, who stomp in puddles and ruin their new pants, who sneak Popsicles before supper, who erase holes in math workbooks, who can never find their shoes.

And we pray for those who stare at photographers from behind barbed wire, who can't bound down the street in a new pair of sneakers, who never "counted potatoes," who are born in places in which we wouldn't be caught dead, who never go to the circus, who live in an X-rated world.

We pray for children who bring us sticky kisses and fistfuls of dandelions, who sleep with the dog and bury goldfish, who hug us in a hurry and forget their lunch money, who cover themselves with Band-Aids and sing off key, who squeeze toothpaste all over the sink, who slurp their soup.

And we pray for those who never get dessert, who have no safe blanket to drag behind them, who watch their parents watch them die, who can't find any bread to steal, who don't have any rooms to clean up, whose pictures aren't on anybody's dresser, whose monsters are real.

We pray for children who spend all their allowance before Tuesday, who throw tantrums in the grocery store and pick their food, who like ghost stories, who shove dirty clothes under the bed and never rinse out the tub, who love visits from the tooth fairy, who don't like to be kissed in front of the school bus, who squirm in church or temple and scream in the phone, whose tears we sometimes laugh at and whose smiles can make us cry.

And we pray for those whose nightmares come in the daytime, who will eat anything, who have never seen a dentist, who aren't spoiled by anybody, who go to bed hungry and cry themselves to sleep. Who live and move and have no being.

We pray for children who want to be carried and for those who must, for those we never give up on and for those who don't get a second chance. For those we smother... and for those who will grab the hand of anyone kind enough to offer it.

Hear our cries, Adonai, and listen to our prayers. Amen.

Ina J. Hughs

Silent Prayer

Dear God: It is wonderful to be alive.
I have been given many blessings:
Food to eat, clothes to wear, people who love me.
Thank You, God,
For all of my wonderful blessings.

Yihyu l'ratzon	יִהְיוּ לְרָצוֹן
imrei fi,	אִמְרֵי־פִי
v'hegyon libi	וְהֶגְיוֹן לִבִּי
l'fanecha,	לְפָנֶיךָ,
Adonai, tzuri v'go-ali.	יהוה, צוּרִי וְגוֹאֲלִי.

May the words of my mouth and the thoughts in my heart be pleasing to You, O God.

Aleinu I

Please rise

Aleinu l'shabei-ach	עָלֵינוּ לְשַׁבֵּחַ
la-adon hakol,	לַאֲדוֹן הַכּל,
lateit g'dula	לָתֵת גְּדֻלָּה
l'yotzeir b'reishit,	לְיוֹצֵר בְּרֵאשִׁית,
shelo asanu	שֶׁלֹּא עָשָׂנוּ
k'goyei ha-aratzot,	כְּגוֹיֵי הָאֲרָצוֹת,
v'lo samanu	וְלֹא שָׂמָנוּ
k'mishp'chot	כְּמִשְׁפְּחוֹת
ha-adama;	הָאֲדָמָה,
shelo sam	שֶׁלֹּא שָׂם
chelkeinu kahem,	חֶלְקֵנוּ כָּהֶם,
v'goraleinu	וְגֹרָלֵנוּ
k'chol hamonam.	כְּכָל הֲמוֹנָם.
Va-anachnu kor'im	וַאֲנַחְנוּ כּוֹרְעִים
umishtachavim	וּמִשְׁתַּחֲוִים
umodim	וּמוֹדִים,
lifnei melech	לִפְנֵי מֶלֶךְ,
malchei ham'lachim,	מַלְכֵי הַמְּלָכִים,
ha-Kadosh	הַקָּדוֹשׁ
Baruch Hu.	בָּרוּךְ הוּא.

We pray that some day the world will be at peace. Then everyone will be free to pray to only You, God. May that great time come soon.

V'ne-emar:	וְנֶאֱמַר:
v'haya Adonai	וְהָיָה יהוה
l'melech	לְמֶלֶךְ
al kol ha-aretz.	עַל־כָּל־הָאָרֶץ;
Bayom hahu	בַּיּוֹם הַהוּא
yihyeh Adonai echad	יִהְיֶה יהוה אֶחָד
ush'mo echad.	וּשְׁמוֹ אֶחָד.

DEAR GOD,

THERE ARE TIMES WHEN EACH OF US FEELS LOST OR ALONE, ADRIFT AND FORSAKEN, UNABLE TO REACH THOSE NEXT TO US OR BE REACHED BY THEM AND THERE ARE DAYS AND NIGHTS WHEN EXISTENCE SEEMS TO LACK ALL PURPOSE, AND OUR LIVES SEEM BRIEF SPARKS IN AN INDIFFERENT COSMOS.

by Tom Fehr

Kaddish

At this time, we think about people who have died.
Some were our family.
Some were our friends.
When we think about these people, we miss them.
We are grateful for memories of them.
We thank You, God, for life and for the people we have loved.

Yitgadal v'yitkadash	יִתְגַּדַּל וְיִתְקַדַּשׁ
sh'mei raba	שְׁמֵהּ רַבָּא.
b'alma di v'ra	בְּעָלְמָא דִּי בְרָא
chir'utei, v'yamlich	כִרְעוּתֵהּ, וְיַמְלִיךְ
malchutei b'chayeichon	מַלְכוּתֵהּ בְּחַיֵּיכוֹן
uv'yomeichon uv'chayei	וּבְיוֹמֵיכוֹן וּבְחַיֵּי
dechol beit Yisra-eil,	דְכָל בֵּית יִשְׂרָאֵל.
ba-agala uviz'man kariv,	בַּעֲגָלָא וּבִזְמַן קָרִיב
v'imru: Amein.	וְאִמְרוּ אָמֵן:
Y'hei sh'mei raba	יְהֵא שְׁמֵהּ רַבָּא
m'varach l'alam	מְבָרַךְ לְעָלַם
ul'almei almaya.	וּלְעָלְמֵי עָלְמַיָּא:
Yitbarach v'yishtabach,	יִתְבָּרַךְ וְיִשְׁתַּבַּח,
v'yitpa-ar v'yitromam	וְיִתְפָּאַר וְיִתְרוֹמַם
v'yitnasei,	וְיִתְנַשֵּׂא
v'yithadar v'yit-aleh v'yithalal	וְיִתְהַדָּר וְיִתְעַלֶּה וְיִתְהַלָּל
sh'mei d'kud'sha,	שְׁמֵהּ דְּקֻדְשָׁא
b'rich hu,	בְּרִיךְ הוּא
l'eila min kol birchata	לְעֵלָּא מִן כָּל בִּרְכָתָא
v'shirata,	וְשִׁירָתָא,
tushb'chata v'nechemata	תֻּשְׁבְּחָתָא וְנֶחֱמָתָא,
da-amiran b'alma,	דַּאֲמִירָן בְּעָלְמָא,
ve-im'ru: Amein.	וְאִמְרוּ אָמֵן:
Y'hei sh'lama raba	יְהֵא שְׁלָמָא רַבָּא
min sh'maya	מִן שְׁמַיָּא
v'chayim aleinu	וְחַיִּים עָלֵינוּ
v'al kol Yisra-eil,	וְעַל כָּל יִשְׂרָאֵל,
v'im'ru: Amein.	וְאִמְרוּ אָמֵן:
Oseh shalom bim'romav,	עֹשֶׂה שָׁלוֹם בִּמְרוֹמָיו
hu ya-aseh shalom	הוּא יַעֲשֶׂה שָׁלוֹם
aleinu v'al kol Yisra-eil,	עָלֵינוּ וְעַל כָּל יִשְׂרָאֵל,
ve-im'ru: Amein.	וְאִמְרוּ אָמֵן:

Closing Song

Hashkiveinu,	הַשְׁכִּיבֵנוּ,
Adonai Eloheinu,	יְיָ אֱלֹהֵינוּ,
L'shalom,	לְשָׁלוֹם,
V'ha-amideinu,	וְהַעֲמִידֵנוּ,
Malkeinu, l'shalom	מַלְכֵּנוּ, לְחַיִּים.

Ufros aleynu sukat shlomecha, ufros eleynu sukat shlomecha. Amen

Shelter us beneath thy wings, O Lord on high.
Guard us from all harmful things, O Lord on high.
Keep us safe throughout the night, till we wake with morning's light.
Teach us GOD wrong from right. Amen.

ONE CHILD PLUS ONE CHILD PLUS ONE...

Sample Jewish Sermon for Children's Shabbat by Rabbi Michael Zedek,
Senior Rabbi, Temple B'nai Jehudah, St. Louis, Mo.

I believe it was Elie Wiesel who offers an engaging interpretation of the first words of Genesis, our book of starting, beginning. *Bereshit bara*— "In the beginning God created"—allows the insight that God created beginnings; the rest God left to us. Alternatively, while God exclusively provides the Start (the beginning), we have a unique capacity, an opportunity: Namely, we can begin again.

So with the challenges for families and especially for our children, let us note the difficulties and the possibilities, but most especially let us commit to do better, to begin again, again.

Abraham Joshua Heschel, z.l., points out that we may not be redeemed (or restore the world's wholeness, or save every child), but at least we should be worthy of being redeemed. May our works, our efforts, testify to that commitment absolutely.

The reference to Heschel suggests two stories with which you may be familiar. The first recalls a time from Heschel's youth when he was studying *Akedat Yitzhak* (the binding of Isaac). As Heschel describes, he began to cry as he read the horrific moment when Abraham raises the knife to slay Isaac. The teacher tried to comfort him. "Don't worry. The angel will stop the knife." To which Heschel responded, "But what if the angel had come too late?"

At a time when angelology has a new currency, it may be instructive to recall that the word is based on the Hebrew for messenger. So we too are supposed to be *melachim*/angels/messengers. And we must not forget that our message needs to be that every child, every person is precious. How do we do that, better live that, if not in concrete deeds, *mitzvot?* So may our prayers translate into such action, and may we not be too late.

Now to the second story, for one obstacle to our engagement often seems to be the enormity and intractability of the challenges before us. After all, what can one person, one congregation, one community do? Well, recall the time-worn tale of a shoreline crowded with marooned starfish as a child walks along the beach throwing into the water as many as he can. A more experienced and, alas, cynical adult cautions, "Why bother? You can't save them all. You can't make any real difference." Undeterred, the child throws back another. "Mister," he declares, "it makes a difference to that one." One child plus one child plus one...

Jewish tradition instructs that one may not live in a town without a physician. And while we may not all be physicians, all have a role to play as healers. For we can bring relief to those in need, and that notion includes all of us, maybe even a healing for us. For in a world of affluence and avarice, any sensitive soul knows that pursuing the good life is never enough. We must also and always be good to life. To call upon Heschel again, he points out that all animals are satisfied when their needs are met. The only exception is humanity. For only we have a need to be a need, to be needed. And who needs/who doesn't need us—the child, so many children, broken and fractured families, even those who are doing well can also do more, can do better. And we can help!

No matter our own family constellation, all have a stake in the future. Consider the Talmudic tale of the carob tree and its generations-long delay before fruit may be harvested. Just as we inherited a world that was cultivated, so should we all be concerned and, even more significantly, engaged in providing deep roots and strong wings for a next generation and more.

A story. One Yom Kippur the great Hasidic master Levi Yitzhak of Berdichev announced that at the conclusion of the fast day he would reveal the secret phrase that would finally usher in the messianic age. With the end of the service, the congregation was enthusiastic as the Rabbi mounted the rostrum. But just as he was about to begin, a child cried out in hunger. So it was that Levi Yitzhak declared, "Feed the child. The Messiah can wait. A hungry child can't wait."

And Jewish tradition would insist that feeding, saving, caring for, providing the right ingredients and the right start for just one child brings redemption closer. One child plus one child plus one...And should we, perhaps, not be redeemed, at least we would be worthy.

The confluence of this Children's Sabbath observance at or near Simchat Torah affords an intriguing connection. For the conclusion of Deuteronomy finds the people on the threshold of the Promised Land. And even as we stand, as did they, on the shoulders of giants, it is easy, too easy, to complain that all around us (in us) is an experience of wilderness. The daily headlines offer more than sufficient testimony about *midbar*/a shifting desert of desperation and danger. It is harder, perhaps, and certainly more important to take the necessary steps on the journey that will make our world better, that will bring us closer to what it is meant to be, closer to a Promised place, a land that is sure and safe for children everywhere. But talk is not (ever) enough. *Lo hamidrash haikar eleh hama'aseh.* Deeds, deeds as we turn to the place where we, where all, begin, *Bereshit barah.* May we begin again!

So an additional story. A deeply troubled student comes to his rabbi. "Rabbi, it's terrible."

"What is, my child?"

"Rabbi, the world is in terrible shape. Why, sometimes I even think I could have made a better world myself."

"My child, that is exactly why God put you here. Now get to work."

For after the service, the worship (the *avodah*/work) really begins.

One final offering from reflections by the philosopher, theologian, and Holocaust survivor Dr. Emil Fackenheim. He describes his early training with a Marxist mentor in pre-Nazi Germany. They were studying birth ceremonies of various ancient peoples as the instructor explained that these rituals represent the superstitious responses of ignorant and primitive minds. Where they saw the intervention of the divine, even something miraculous, we know that the birth is nothing more than a perfectly natural process. But the Holocaust convinced Fackenheim that anyone who doesn't recognize that a child is nothing less than a miracle doesn't deserve a child.

May our gathering bring proof that we recognize miracles and that we deserve (even as we are here to serve) children everywhere.

Jewish Lesson Plans

The following Jewish Lesson Plans are designed for a one-hour class. They may be used instead of your regular curriculum on the Children's Shabbat, incorporated into your curriculum, or used during a special Children's Shabbat educational session on the Children's Shabbat weekend or on a weekend or weeknight preceding the Children's Shabbat.

Several of the lesson plans have activities with end products that can be shared with the whole congregation, such as a mural or a dramatic presentation. Decide in advance how and when these results might be shared with the congregation. Will you present them after the education hour or after the service on the day of your Children's Shabbat? Will you extend the focus on children in need and share the created end products the following week? Or you may want to use these lessons the week before the Children's Shabbat so that, for example, the dramatic presentation could be incorporated into the Children's Shabbat service.

Please note: Whenever you raise problems facing children, there is the possibility that your own students are facing some of these concerns themselves. This calls for two kinds of preparation. First, you want to be sensitive to the students so they don't feel embarrassed or ashamed if you are talking about a problem that they are facing themselves. Second, you need to be prepared to respond to disclosures that may be prompted by the discussion, such as a conversation about children who are being hurt by a grown-up. Know in advance how you would respond to a disclosure and what resources you would turn to, such as the rabbi or a child welfare hotline. Contact a director of an early childhood program or after-school program, a scout leader, or the local office of child welfare for information on how to get help in your community. Please don't let this caution deter you from raising these topics; just be prepared. You may end up making more of a difference in the life of a child than you could have imagined.

Lesson Plan for Preschool Children (ages 3-4)

Theme

God made everything and everyone. Because every child is made by God, every child is good and important to God. We can help care for other children, as God's helpers.

Lesson Objectives

The students will:

- Learn about Simchat Torah and its return to the beginning of the Torah.
- Hear the creation story, with an emphasis on God's creation being good.
- Think about themselves and other children as part of God's good creation.
- Participate in an active response to help other children who are part of God's good creation.

Materials

- Storybook version of the creation story
- Creation story felt board and felt shapes, or construction paper shapes (white paper "light," black paper "dark," waters, sky, land, seas, plants, sun and moon, fish and birds, cows and lions, man and woman or boy and girl)
- Coloring paper with heading "I Am Part of God's Good World!," one piece per child
- Crayons or markers
- Optional: stickers of plants, animals, sun and moon
- Pictures cut from magazines featuring nurse or doctor, teacher, parent, babysitter, police officer, rabbi (parenting magazines may be good sources for such pictures)
- Construction paper and glue for mounting magazine pictures

Preparation

- Review page 88.
- Review lesson and gather materials.
- Practice retelling creation story with felt board or construction paper shapes.
- Prepare headings on coloring paper for children.
- Cut pictures (noted above) from magazines and glue onto construction paper, one picture per piece.

Overview

1. Opening and Introduction of Theme (5 minutes)
2. Story of Creation (10 minutes)
3. Explore the Theme (Activities, Discussion) (40 minutes)
4. Closing (5 minutes)

1. Opening and Introduction of Theme

Guide a discussion, using the questions and making the points below:

- Who has a favorite book or video?
- Do you read it or watch it over and over?
- The Torah contains stories that are read over and over. They are read every year.
- After you finish reading your favorite book, when you want to read it again you go back to the first page, to the beginning. After you finish watching your favorite video, when you want to watch it again, you have to rewind it and go back to the beginning. Every year, the Torah has a new beginning, too. It is a special day called *Simchat Torah*. When the Torah has a new beginning each year, we go back to the very first story in the Torah.

2. Story of Creation

If you are teaching older children, ask, "Does anyone know what the first story in the Torah is about? Who can tell me what happens in the beginning of the Torah?"

Explain that the first story in the beginning of the Torah is about God making the world—all of the animals, plants and trees, and people. The *beginning* of the Torah is a story about the *beginning* of the world! (If a Torah is in the room, show where the first portion is.)

Read or tell the story of creation, using a very short version for pre-k children. Emphasize the goodness of God's creation, and God's charge to us to help care for the world.

Retell the creation story using a felt board and felt shapes, or holding up construction paper cut-outs for each part of the story. Ask the children what God made each day, holding up the shapes to remind them. Invite the children to respond to each stage of the story by saying together "And it was good!" At the end, ask, "Did God ask the plants to help take care of the world?" *(No.)* "Did God ask the animals to help take care of the world?" *(No.)* "Who did God ask to help take care of the world?" *(People.)*

3. Explore the Theme

Coloring Activity (10 minutes)

Remind the children, "God made everyone and everything, and God said that everything God made is good! You are part of God's good world." Distribute papers with the heading "I Am Part of God's Good World!" along with crayons or markers. Invite the children to draw pictures of themselves. Add their names. If desired, you can also distribute stickers of plants, animals, sun, moon, and stars for the children to add to their pictures. Arrange to display the pictures in the temple building.

Discussion: Children Need Different Kinds of Help (10 minutes)

Gather the children back together. Remind the children that God wants people to help take care of each other and the rest of God's world. Ask the following questions, allowing time for responses. "What are ways that you are a helper? Who has a pet? How do you help take care of your pet? Who helps your mommy or daddy when they are working in the yard? Do you help rake leaves or dig in the dirt? Who has a baby sister or brother? How do you help take care of your baby sister or brother?

Say, "Everyone can be a helper. And everyone needs to be helped in some way, at some time. Mommies need help. Daddies need help. Teachers need help."

"Some children face extra hard problems that need our help.

"Some children are sick or hurt, and need to visit a doctor. If you have been to a doctor, raise your hand. Isn't it good to have someone to help us get better?

"Some children need a safe place to be while their parents are working. Who takes care of you during the day? *(Allow children to respond. Answers may include parents, grandparents, babysitters, child care teachers.)* Doesn't it feel good to have people to take good care of you and help you learn and have fun?

"Some children don't have enough food to eat or warm clothes to wear or a place to live. How does it feel to be hungry? *(Allow time for response.)* It's not a very good feeling, is it? Everyone is hungry some time, but some children are hungry a lot of the time because their parents don't have enough money to buy food."

Discussion: How Could You Help? (10 minutes)

Say, "Let's think of ways that we can help other children who need our help." Then ask the following questions, allowing the children time to respond to each.

- How could you help someone who fell down on the playground and was crying?
- How could you help someone who was hungry and didn't have any lunch to eat?
- How could you help someone who was cold and didn't have any mittens or a coat?
- How could you help someone who didn't know whether to lie or tell the truth? Who wanted to take something that didn't belong to them?

Affirm their responses, saying "Those are good ways that you can help take care of other people the way God wants us to."

Activity: Grown-Ups Who Help (10 minutes)

For this activity, hold up the prepared pictures and, for each, ask the children how this person is a helper and how they help children. Be open to a range of responses. First, hold up a picture of a nurse or a doctor. Next, hold up a picture of a teacher, parent, or babysitter. Next, a picture of someone who helps those who are poor or hungry. Next, show a picture of a police officer. Finally, show a picture of a rabbi or teacher.

Alternative: Lay the pictures on a table or on the floor or hang on a bulletin board. Ask the children to help you identify people who are helpers. There may be more than one right answer.

- Who helps children when they are sick?
- Who helps children learn at school or day care?
- Who takes care of children at home?
- Who helps children when someone hurts them?
- Who helps children when they are hungry?
- Who helps children learn about God?

4. Closing

Have the children come back to a closing circle. Ask them to repeat the following prayer:
"Dear God,
thank you for the grown-ups
who are our helpers.
Help us to be good helpers, too."

Lesson Plan for the Elementary Grades

(with adaptations for grades K-2 and grades 3-5)

Theme

God created everyone and everything good, and charged us to help care for creation. We can take care of God's good creation by helping children in need.

Lesson Objectives

The students will:
- Recall the meaning of Simchat Torah.
- Review the creation story and consider its emphasis on the goodness of creation and call to care for creation.
- Learn about children in need and reflect on ways that they can care for other children.
- Participate in an active response to help care for children in need.

Materials

- Storybook version of the creation story, preferably one that emphasizes the goodness of God's creation and the charge to care for creation
- Index cards
- Large bowl
- Please see activity options in *Respond to the Theme*, and gather the materials noted in the activity or activities you select.

Preparation

- Review page 88.
- Read through the lesson and gather the materials required.
- Practice telling the story.
- Familiarize yourself with the material in the discussion in *Explore the Theme*. Alternatively, find pictures for each of the sections (for example, a child who is hurt, a child who looks scared, a child with a caregiver). Parenting magazines may be good sources for such pictures. Cut out the pictures, and paste each one on a separate piece of paper. On the back of the paper, write the information and questions provided for each section. During the discussion you can hold up the picture for the children to see, while you refresh your memory by reading what you have written on the back.
- Write the grab bag questions on index cards (one for each student) and put them in the bowl. Make up additional questions if needed. (Don't write out the "start" headings, which are simply provided to help you see the range of topics addressed.)

- Please see activity options in *Respond to the Theme*, and conduct any preparation noted in the activity or activities you select.

Overview

1. Introduce the Theme and Torah Story (10 minutes)
2. Explore the Theme (Discussion, Grab Bag Questions, Game) (30 minutes)
3. Respond to the Theme (15 minutes)
4. Closing (1-5 minutes)

1. Introduce the Theme and Torah Story

Say, "Today is a special day for two different reasons. First, it is a special Jewish holiday. Can anyone tell me what holiday it is? *(Simchat Torah.)* Today is special for a second reason. It is Children's Shabbat, a special day when our congregation looks for ways that we can help other children, such as children who are sick, or hungry, or scared, or don't have someone to take care of them when their parents are at work."

Say, "On Simchat Torah, we finish reading the Torah scroll, and return to the beginning. Does anyone remember the very first story in the beginning of the Torah?" *(Allow children to respond. Supply the correct answer if students do not.)*

Read the storybook version of the creation story.

YOUNGER ELEMENTARY VERSION: For younger children, you may want to reinforce the story by retelling it using a flannel board and felt shapes or construction paper shapes you have cut out. (Please see directions in Preschool Lesson Plan.) Encourage the children to join in the refrain "And it was good!" at the conclusion of each day's creation.

OLDER ELEMENTARY VERSION: For older children, you may want to ask questions such as "Were some of the things God created not so good or only sort of good?" *(No.)* "So that means every single person and every single thing created by God is good and important to God?" *(Yes.)* "Did God ask the plants to help take care of the world?" *(No.)* "Did God ask the birds or fish or cows or wild animals to help take care of the world?" *(No.)* "Who did God give the special and important job to of helping take care of the world?" *(People.)*

Say, "God created people to be God's partners in creation. What does it mean to be a partner? *(Allow students time to respond.)* When we create something, we also like to take care of it and protect it. We serve as God's partner when we take care of and protect all of God's creations."

Say, "In class today, we are going to talk about taking care of other children, and do a project to help other children."

2. Explore the Theme

Discussion: Children Who Need Our Help
(10 minutes)

YOUNGER ELEMENTARY VERSION:

Ask, "Who needs to be helped in some way, at some time?" *(Accept the answers they come up with. Add mothers, fathers, teachers, rabbis, and children, if the children do not offer these answers.)*

Say, "Some children face extra hard problems that need our help."

Continue, "Some children are sick or hurt, and need to visit a doctor. Raise your hand if you have ever been to the doctor." *(Allow time for a show of hands.)* "When children are sick or hurt, it is important to have someone who can help them get better. Children need a Healthy Start."

Say, "Some children need a safe place to be while their parents are working. Who takes care of you after school?" *(Allow children to respond. Answers may include parents, grandparents, babysitters.)* "Doesn't it feel good to have people to take good care of you? Children need the Head Start of good, loving care."

Say, "Some children don't have enough food to eat or warm clothes to wear or a place to live. How does it feel to be hungry?" *(Allow time for responses.)* "It's not a very good feeling, is it? Everyone is hungry some time, but some children are hungry a lot of the time because their parents don't have enough money to buy food. It's not fair that some children are hungry. All children need a Fair Start."

Say, "Some children are scared because they don't feel safe. They are worried about being hurt by someone. Have you ever been scared? What are some of the things that help you feel safe?" *(Answers may include a parent or adult, a toy, a pet, a friend.)* "All children need a Safe Start."

Say, "Who are some of the people who help you know the difference between what is right and what is wrong, and help you do the right thing? Who are some of the people who help you learn about God? *(If children need further guidance,*

you may want to ask them about any of the following: parents, older brothers and sisters, teachers, religious school teachers, and the rabbi.) Say, "It is important to have people who can help us learn to do the right thing. Children need a Moral Start."

Conclude, "There are lots of people who can help children. There are parents and grandparents and doctors and teachers and school nurses and police officers and rabbis and babysitters and more. Who else can help children? *(Allow time for responses.)* You know who else can help children? You can!"

OLDER ELEMENTARY VERSION
With older students, you may want to have a more open-ended discussion than the guided discussion above. If so, use the opening questions noted below, and then tailor your responses based on what the children come up with. If students provide openings, try to underscore the five major areas of children's health, child care, poverty, violence, and the need for moral guidance/learning to do the right thing.

Ask, "Who needs to be helped in some way, at some time?" *(Accept the answers they come up with. Add mothers, fathers, teachers, rabbis, and children, if the children do not offer these answers.)*

Say, "Some children face extra hard problems that need our help. What hard problems do some children have?"

Depending on their answers, use responses like these:

"When children are really sick or hurt, it is important to be able to see a doctor to help them get better. It's also important to be able to see a doctor for check-ups to help children stay healthy. All children need a Healthy Start."

"When children need a safe place to be, it feels good to have people take care of them, like parents or babysitters. Children need a Head Start of good, loving care."

"When children want to learn about all kinds of things, they need the Head Start of good schools and teachers that keep them excited about learning and being the very best students they can be."

"When children don't have enough food to eat (or warm clothes to wear or a place to live) they need help. It's not fair that some children are hungry most of the time, or don't have a place to live. All children need a Fair Start."

"When children are scared because they don't feel safe or because they are being hurt, they need someone to help them feel safe. All children need a Safe Start."

"When children don't know whether to lie or tell the truth, they need friends and parents who can encourage them to do the right thing. All children need a Moral Start."

"When children are worried they won't do well on a test, and are tempted to cheat, they need friends and family who tell them that it is more important to be honest and do the right thing than to get a high grade on a test. All children need a Moral Start."

Grab Bag Questions: How Could You Help?
(10 minutes)

Have the children take turns picking an index card out of the bowl and answering the question written on it. (Provide assistance reading the question, as needed, with younger children.) Once the child who picked the question has responded, other children may volunteer additional ideas. Remind the children that there are some situations that children can't handle by themselves, and the best way to help then is by getting an adult to help, too.

Grab Bag Questions

Children need a Healthy Start:
- How could you help someone who hurt herself on the playground during recess?
- How could you help someone who is sick but whose parents don't have money to take him to the doctor?
- How could you help someone who is having trouble seeing the chalkboard but hasn't told anyone?

Children need a Head Start:
- How could you help someone who is scared to stay home alone after school, but doesn't have anywhere to go?
- How could you help someone who doesn't have anyone to help her with her homework?

Children need a Fair Start:
- How could you help someone who is hungry and doesn't have any lunch?
- How could you help someone who doesn't have a warm winter coat and whose parents don't have money to buy one?
- How could you help someone who is being teased about not having a telephone or computer at her house because her parents don't have the money?

- How could you help someone who is being teased about not having the "cool" kind of sneakers because he couldn't afford them?

Children need a Safe Start:
- How could you help someone who is being hurt by a grown-up?
- How could you help someone who is scared to walk home because her neighborhood is dangerous and has a lot of fighting?
- How could you help someone who is angry at someone else?
- How could you help someone who was told he'll be beaten up after school?
- How could you help someone who wants to show you the gun her parents own?

Children need a Moral Start:
- How could you help someone who told a lie because she is worried about getting into trouble?
- How could you help someone who has a question about God?
- How could you help someone who wants to steal something from a store?
- How could you help someone who wants to do something you know is wrong?

Affirm the students' responses as they are offered, with comments like "You would be taking good care of someone if you did that," or "I think that's just the kind of help God wants us to give people." If a student proposes an inappropriate idea, you might say, "I can tell you really care about trying to help someone who has a problem," and, as needed, offer assistance redirecting the solution.

Game: Helping Each Other (10 minutes)
Pair the children up (designating one in each pair as "A" and the other as "B"). Have them line up on one side of the room, and indicate the "finish line" on the other side of the room. (You may choose to go outside or to another place in the synagogue if there is not enough space in your classroom.) For the first round, tell the children that they must cross the room, but the A's cannot use one foot, and the B's must close their eyes. The children in each pair must help each other to cross the room. Affirm even the last pair to cross the line, saying "Remember, what is most important is helping take care of each other, not who is first." For the second round, tell the A's that they must walk backwards (with B's keeping them from walking into other

children), and the B's must hop on one foot (holding on to A's for balance). Again, affirm that the process of helping each other was more important than who crossed the line first. Make up a few more rounds, if time and interest permit.

3. Respond to the Theme

Select one of the following projects (or several, if you want to set up activity centers):

- **In honor of Simchat Torah's emphasis on the importance of learning for a lifetime, plan a book drive to collect books to donate to programs serving children in need.** The books could be given to a hospital, a social service agency, a community health clinic, or a homeless shelter serving families. Have the students brainstorm ways they can collect the books. Possibilities include decorating boxes to be placed in the synagogue building, and asking members to bring in books to donate; selecting one of their own books in good condition to give; or raising money to buy books through a "read-a-thon," in which parents and others pledge a certain amount (such as a quarter or a dollar) for every book on a subject of Jewish interest that the student reads in the next month. Have supplies on hand so the students can begin decorating collection boxes, designing a pledge form, making posters announcing the book drive, or taking other actions. (Note: This activity is also suggested in the middle school lesson plan. You may want to coordinate this with the middle school teacher and students.) Alternatively, the children could make their own picture books of the creation story to give to the preschool class or to a program serving young children. Either assign a child or small group of children one day to illustrate, and collect them together into one book, or have each child prepare her own book. You may write out the text for younger children; for older children, help them copy the actual text or an appropriate paraphrase. Laminating the finished pages or covering them with clear adhesive paper will increase the books' durability. The pages could be illustrated with crayons and markers or with collages created by using pictures cut from magazines.

- **Have the children decorate brown paper bags that will be filled with items to be distributed at a food pantry serving families.** Have them use materials such as crayons, markers, pictures cut from magazines, and stickers. While they are working, talk with them about children who are hungry, and how those children will feel when the bag is filled with good food to eat. *Optional:* Ask each child to bring in a non-perishable food item (such as peanut butter or ravioli in a

can) the next week to put in the bags. If there is extra time, have the children make friendly cards to tuck into each bag. An alternative would be to fill the bags with baby care items, such as diapers, diaper wipes, baby food, baby shampoo and soap.

- **Have the children make "Feel Better" cards for children in the hospital.** Contact the pediatric wing of a local hospital in advance, and get the names of children who would appreciate receiving cards. Give each child an 8½" x 11" piece of paper folded in half and then in half again to form a blank card. Guide the students in writing appropriate messages inside, and then have them decorate the front and back with crayons, markers, or stickers. While they are working, talk with them about children who are hurt and sick. Note that some children can't even see a doctor when they are sick because their parents don't have enough money. Affirm that your students are being good helpers and that some sick children will feel better when they receive the cards. (If there is extra time, the children could make drawings to decorate a waiting room of your community's health clinic.)

- **Have the children come up with a "Peacemaker Plan" that lists steps to reduce violence and keep children safe.** Have younger children dictate their plans to you to write down on posterboard; older children can write theirs out themselves. Both groups can illustrate the poster. Suggest scenarios and have them come up with several ideas for each: "If you are feeling angry at someone you can help by..." "If you see two children having a fight you can help by..." "If you are someplace where there is a gun (at school, at a friend's house, etc.) you can help by..." "If someone you know is being hurt by a grown-up, you can help by..."

4. Closing

Gather the children in a circle for your closing time. Ask the children to think about a time when someone helped them. Tell them you are going to begin the prayer and will give them a chance to add their own. Begin by saying, "Thank you, God, for people who have helped us. Thank you for *(add your own example)*." Then, invite the children to add their own "thank you's" to God for a time they were helped. End the prayer by saying, "Help us to help other people. Amen."

Lesson Plan for Middle School (Grades 6, 7, & 8)

Theme

On Simchat Torah, we celebrate returning to the beginning of the Torah, where we read the story of God's good creation and God's charge to us to care for creation. On this Children's Shabbat, there are many ways we can help take care of children in need who are part of God's good creation, and give them the good beginning they need.

Lesson Objectives

The students will:
- Understand the significance of Simchat Torah.
- Recall the story of creation and our responsibility to help take care of God's good creation.
- Think about ways that they can help take care of children in need (who are part of God's good creation) and give them a good new beginning.

Materials

- Supplies for the chosen activity in *Respond to the Theme*.

Preparation

- Review page 88.
- Preparation for the chosen activity in *Respond to the Theme*.

Overview

1. Opening and Introduction of the Theme (10 minutes)
2. Explore the Theme: Put Yourself in Their Shoes (20 minutes)
3. Respond to the Theme (20 minutes)
4. Closing (10 minutes)

1. Opening and Introduction of the Theme

Ask the students what Jewish holiday it is. Ask them to explain Simchat Torah's significance. Correct or add to the answers as necessary. Ask what the first story in the Torah is. Remind the students that God created everything good, and that God charged human beings with responsibility for helping care for all of creation.

Say, "On Simchat Torah, we celebrate the good beginning of the Torah. On this Children's Shabbat, we also think about the good beginning that every child needs in life:

- Children need the Healthy Start of good health care, so they can see a doctor when they are sick or hurt, and for regular check-ups to keep them healthy.
- Children need a Head Start of loving people who take care of them in their families, schools, and after school.
- Children need a Fair Start of enough food to eat, a place to live, and jobs for their parents so they can provide for them.
- Children need a Safe Start of homes, schools, and communities that are free from violence and where people resolve their conflicts peacefully.
- And children need a Moral Start, where families and congregations help them develop good values and make good choices in life.

"These are good starts in life that are important year after year, just as the Torah has a good beginning year after year." [Alternative: lay out this list as a handout, and ask a different student to read about each "start."]

2. Explore the Theme: Put Yourself in Their Shoes

Say, "Since most of us have had these 'good starts' in life, it can be hard to imagine what it is like for the children who have not had these starts. We are going to do an activity called 'Put Yourself In Their Shoes' that will help us think about children who don't have the starts they need in life."

Have the students line up. Outline a circle in another part of the room, either by using children's shoes which you have brought in (or asked the students to bring in) or by putting down masking tape. Tell the students, "We are going to learn about some of the problems facing children across our nation by 'putting ourselves in their shoes.' I am going to ask questions about some statistics (or 'numbers'). When I tell you the statistic, like 'one out of every four,' let's have every fourth person move into the circle."

Then, using the statistics in "Put Yourself in Their Shoes," have the students separate themselves accordingly. For example, say, "Do you know how many preschoolers have a mother who works, and need someone else to take care of them, like a relative, child care center, or babysitter?" Say, "One out of every two preschoolers needs some kind of child care." Then, every other student (i.e., one in two) should move into the designated circle. Encourage them to figure out how to group themselves accurately, but guide them if necessary. Then, ask the students to get back into a line. Say, "Do you know how many children will be poor at some point in their childhood?" Say, "One out of every three children will be poor at some point in their childhood." Then every third student should move into the circle. Continue with the rest of the statistics.

At the end of the exercise, ask the students to share their reaction. Which statistics surprised them the most? What do they think about the problems described? What do they think they should do? What do they think the synagogue, community, or government should do?

3. Respond to the Theme

Select one or more of the following activities.

- **In honor of Simchat Torah's emphasis on the importance of learning for a lifetime, plan a book drive to collect books to donate to programs serving children in need.** The books could be given to a hospital, a social service agency, a community health clinic, or a homeless shelter serving families. Have the students brainstorm ways they can collect the books. Possibilities include decorating boxes to be placed in the synagogue building, and asking members to bring in books to donate; selecting one of their own books in good condition to give; or raising money to buy books through a "read-a-thon," in which parents and others pledge a certain amount (such as a quarter or a dollar) for every book on a subject of Jewish interest that the student reads in the next month. Have supplies on hand so the students can begin decorating collection boxes, designing a pledge form, making posters announcing the book drive, or taking other actions. (Note: This activity is also suggested in the elementary lesson plan. You may want to coordinate this with the elementary teacher and students.) Alternatively, the children could make their own picture books of the creation story to give to the preschool class or to a program serving young children. Either assign a child or small group of children one day to illustrate, and collect them together into one book, or have each child prepare their own book. You may write out the text for younger children; for older children, help

them copy the actual text or an appropriate paraphrase. Laminating the finished pages or covering them with clear adhesive paper will increase the books' durability. The pages could be illustrated with crayons and markers or with collages created by using pictures cut from magazines.

- **Contribute to a child-serving organization.** Plan a project to collect money or needed items to donate to an organization serving children and families in the community. In honor of Simchat Torah, it could be an organization that helps children learn, such as an after-school tutoring program. If possible, identify before class the organization to which the class will give, and find out what needs they have in addition to money (such as school supplies, educational games and toys, or educational computer programs). During class, have the students brainstorm how they will raise the money or collect the items. Possibilities include a bake sale, car wash, and raking leaves. Pick a date for the fund-raising effort and list the steps the class will need to complete to make it a success, such as publicizing it through posters, flyers, and other announcements.

- **Make it a sweet beginning.** Make sweets to eat and to donate to a program serving children. Prepare cards to send along with the sweets. Another possibility is to attach the treats to the books being donated (see first activity idea), along with cards in which the children inscribe messages such as "Reading is the best treat of all. Enjoy!," or "We hope you have a sweet time reading this book." As the children prepare this activity, tell them of the Jewish tradition of putting honey on the first page of a book to make reading a pleasurable experience for children.

4. Closing

- Review the concepts developed in the lesson.
- Dance the *hora* to show celebration.
- Ask each student to name something they can do in the coming week and in the coming year to bring a feeling of celebration to a child.

PUT YOURSELF IN THEIR SHOES

Children need and deserve a Healthy Start:
- 1 in 6 children has no health insurance.
- 1 in 6 babies is born to a mother who had no prenatal care during the first three months of pregnancy.

Children need and deserve a Head Start:
- 1 in 2 preschoolers has a mother in the labor force.
- 1 in 3 students is a year or more behind in school.
- 1 in 8 students never graduates from high school.

Children need and deserve a Fair Start:
- 1 in 3 children will be poor at some point in childhood.
- 1 in 5 children is poor right now.
- 1 in 5 children lives in a family receiving food stamps.
- 1 in 7 children lives with a working relative but is poor nonetheless.

Children need and deserve a Safe Start:
- Every day, 6 children commit suicide in our nation.
- Every day, 10 children are homicide victims.
- Every day, 12 children are killed by guns.

(Data from *The State of America's Children 2000* by the Children's Defense Fund.)

Lesson Plan for High School (Grades 9-12)

Theme

Children are part of God's good creation. In the creation story, God gives humankind responsibility for helping care for creation. We can work together to give every child the start in life they need and deserve.

Lesson Objectives

The students will:
- Review the creation story and its emphasis on creation's goodness and our stewardship.
- Learn about children in need.
- Participate in active responses to help improve the lives of children.

Materials

- Copies of the Hebrew and English translation of the creation story, one per student
- Index cards
- Large bowl
- Please see activity options in *Respond to the Theme*, and gather the materials noted in the activity or activities you select.
- Optional: microphone on a microphone stand

Preparation

- Review page 88.

- Write each of the facts in "Sound Bite Facts" on a separate index card and place in the large bowl. (Don't write out the "start" headings; they are simply to help you see the areas covered.)

- Review activity options in *Respond to the Theme*, and conduct the preparation noted in the activity or activities you select.

Overview

1. Introduce the Theme and Torah Story (15 minutes)
2. Explore the Theme (Sound Bites) (20 minutes)
3. Respond to the Theme (20 minutes)
4. Closing (5 minutes)

1. Introduce the Theme and Torah Story

Tell the students that this weekend marks two significant events—one, a Jewish holiday; the other, an observance across many faith traditions. Ask if anyone can name and explain them. Supplement their responses as necessary. *(The National Observance of Children's Sabbaths is a weekend set aside by Jewish, Christian, and Muslim congregations, and people of other faiths, too, to celebrate children, learn more about the problems facing many children in our nation, reflect on the teachings in every faith to care for and protect children, and commit to action to improve the lives of children.)*

Give each student a copy (both Hebrew and English translation) of the Torah portion for Simchat Torah. After the students have read it (aloud or silently), ask which one word God uses most to describe creation. *("Good.")* Ask if God qualified that, saying that some of creation was only "sort of good," or even "not so good." *(No.)*

Say that today, as Children's Shabbat, the class will be thinking specifically about children as part of God's good creation. Ask, "Do you think we treat every child as part of the good creation, as inherently good? Why or why not? Why do you think we—our nation, community, schools, peers—treat some children as not so good, not so worthwhile?" Have the students come up with a list of children who aren't treated as "good" or "valuable."

If the students don't arrive at the answers by themselves, ask, "Do we treat poor children as part of the good creation? How about those who are struggling in school or have dropped out?" Say, "There are 11.9 million children without health insurance in our nation—they can't see a doctor when they are sick or for check-ups to keep them healthy, because their parents can't afford it. Are those children, who can't see a doctor, being cared for as part of God's good creation?"

2. Explore the Theme: Sound Bites

Ask the students the students to define a "sound bite." (A "sound bite" is a short sentence or two that really catches your attention because it tells you something important or surprising in an interesting way that you are likely to remember.)

Give them one or more of the following examples. (Before class starts, you may want to invite another teacher or students who have arrived early to prepare to read the following examples as if they were radio or TV spots.) "Almost 12 children are killed by guns each day. That is the equivalent of a classroomful of children dying from guns every two days. Let's learn something really important: we've got to work together to stop the violence." "Nearly 1 in 5 children is poor in our nation. While we sit down to dinner tables loaded with good food tonight, one out of every five children in our country may not be sitting down to any dinner at all, or one so small that they still go to bed hungry." "You know how your stomach growls and aches a little sometimes in the class period right before lunch? It sure feels great to get to lunch, doesn't it? Imagine if your stomach felt that hunger all the time, if you never got enough to eat. Well, the nearly 1 in 5 children who are poor in our nation don't just imagine it; they live it every day. Let's do something about it."

Have each student draw an index card with one of the facts below written on it from the bowl. If the class is large, have them work in pairs or repeat some of the facts. Give them five minutes to write a "sound bite" about the fact on their index card, as they would hear in a radio or TV spot. (Encourage them to let you know if they don't fully understand their fact.) Remind them that they want to catch our attention and make us remember their fact. (Tips: comparing a number to something familiar; contrasting circumstances to highlight differences; using vivid, emotional words.)

Sound Bite Facts

Children need a Healthy Start:
11.9 million children don't have health insurance (1 in every 6 children).

Children need a Head Start:
13 million children are in child care, including 6 million babies and toddlers.
1 in 2 preschoolers has a mother who works. 2/3 of mothers of young children work outside the home, many out of economic necessity.

Children need a Fair Start:
13.5 million children are poor (nearly 1 in 5 children).

Children need a Safe Start and a Moral Start:
Almost 12 children are killed by guns each day.
218 children are arrested for violent crimes each day (that is one every 7 minutes).
5,044 children are arrested each day.

After the students have written their sound bites, have them take turns reading them aloud. If you want, you can play a "news anchor" to set it up. (If available, use a microphone on a stand to enhance this activity.) Say, "This is your anchor *[make up a goofy name or use your own]*, bringing you an

important story on the status of children from our reporters in the field. Take it away, *[name of the first student to read]*."

Invite the students to react to what they learned in the sound bites. Which facts surprised them? How do these facts make them feel? Angry? Hopeless? Determined? Sad?

Encourage them to memorize their sound bite and share it with others in the coming week to help raise awareness about children's problems. Emphasize that sound bites can be helpful in calling attention to the problems but that action is needed to make a difference.

3. Respond to the Theme: Activities

Emphasize that we can help solve the problems described in the sound bites. We can serve children in need through raising awareness about the problems, by reaching out to them, and by speaking up on their behalf.

Select one or more of the following activities for your class to do as a whole or in smaller groups.

Serve Children by Raising Awareness

- Have the students make a collage to be displayed in the synagogue to raise awareness. Have them come up with a heading such as "Give Every Child a Good Beginning: A Healthy Start, a Head Start, a Fair Start, a Safe Start, and a Moral Start." Have them write their sound bites on mural paper and add drawings or pictures cut from magazines featuring children, parents and those who help children such as teachers and doctors, prayers, poems, and other thoughts.

- Have them practice the "news report" (perhaps with a student playing the "anchor" this time) to present to the congregation, perhaps during the oneg Shabbat. Alternatively, use a video camera to make a videotape of the newscast to show to the congregation or other religious school classes.

Serve Children by Reaching Out

- Have the students focus on one of the five "starts": a Healthy Start (health), a Head Start (early childhood nurture and education), a Fair Start (child poverty), a Safe Start (safety), or a Moral Start (moral grounding). Next, have them brainstorm the different sources of support or organizations that are meeting the need. For example, a Fair Start (child poverty) might be addressed by the welfare office, a congregational food pantry, a community soup kitchen, Habitat for Humanity, and the agency which distributes housing subsidies, and job training programs. Then, have them brainstorm the kinds of volunteer support and donations they think could be useful. For example, donations could include food, clothing (children's clothes and adult's job interview clothing), books and toys, diapers, and baby items like high chairs and safety gates. Volunteer help might include distributing food at the pantry, playing with children at the welfare office while parents are in line, and building a Habitat house. Encourage them to think about gifts and skills that they have that could be unique contributions. Finally, decide if the class would like to pursue one of these possibilities. You may want to research some organizations beforehand to determine if help is needed. The students could spearhead a collection drive in the congregation to gather the donation items or sign up to volunteer as a group or individually on successive weeks.

Serve Children by Speaking Out

- Have each student write a letter to one of their legislators that describes the problems they have learned about, urges solutions, and asks for a reply. They can use their sound bites in the letters. Give them copies of the sample format in Section 6 in this manual. Be sure to have on hand paper, envelopes, pens, stamps, and the names and addresses of legislators.

- Have them write a similar letter to the editor of your local paper. This could be done as a group letter or individually. They may want to refer to the Children's Shabbat.

4. Closing

- Review the concepts developed in the lesson.
- Ask each student to name something they can do in the coming week and the coming year to bring a feeling of celebration to a child.

Lesson Plan for Adults

Theme

Children are part of God's good creation. In the creation story, God gives humankind responsibility for helping care for creation. We can work together to give every child the start in life they need and deserve.

Lesson Objectives

Participants will:
- Consider a Torah portion and its implications for serving children in need.
- Learn more about the needs of children today.
- Consider ways they can serve children and help to treat them as part of God's good creation.

Materials

- Copies of the Torah portion (Hebrew and English translation)
- Flip chart paper and markers
- Copies of handouts on pages 104-105 and 106
- Pens and pencils
- Copies of the handout "Celebration of Children"

Preparation

- Review the lesson plan.
- Make a copy of the handouts for each participant.

Overview

1. Opening and Introduction to the Theme (15 minutes)
2. Explore the Theme (10 minutes)
3. Respond to the Theme (30 minutes)
4. Closing (5 minutes)

1. Opening and Introduction to the Theme

Welcome participants to the class. Remind them that this weekend is Children's Shabbat, a time when congregations of many faiths across the nation are uniting in a focus on children in need. It is also, of course, Simchat Torah.

Invite participants to turn to the Torah portion that contains the creation story. Have them read through it silently or aloud. When they are done, invite them to respond to the following questions:

- Is there any part of God's creation that was created less than good, or only partially good? What might such an encompassing message of goodness and inherent worth mean for how we treat all children?

- How do you understand the charge to help care for creation? How well do you think we are fulfilling that charge as a congregation, community, or nation when it comes to children? What are signs that we are fulfilling the charge well? What are signs that we are not fulfilling that charge well?

- How do you relate the concept of *Tikkun Olam* to the Genesis passage and to the condition of children in our nation and world?

2. Explore the Theme

Who Is Being Treated as Less Than Good?

Tell the class that even though we regard our own children as inherently good and valuable, there are many children today whose circumstances imply that they are not good, important, and valuable parts of God's creation.

Ask the class to compile a list of the children who are being treated as less than good or valuable parts of God's creation. (For example, "children who are homeless," "children who have been abandoned by both parents.") Record their ideas on flip chart paper.

Distribute copies of the handout "Children Today Are Being Left Behind." Have class members take turns reading paragraphs aloud.

Provide time for people to share their reactions or responses when the reading is complete, especially in light of the Torah portion that was discussed earlier.

3. Respond to the Theme

How Can We Treat All Children as Part of God's Good Creation? What Do They Need?

Tell the class that although there are countless children getting the message that they are not so good or valuable, we can work together to help care for all children and give them the start in life that they need and deserve.

Distribute copies of the handout "Leave No Child Behind." Divide the group into five small groups, if your class is large enough. (Otherwise, divide into fewer small groups or keep the class together and do the brainstorming as one large group.) Assign one of the "starts" to each of the small groups. Ask them to brainstorm ideas for how individuals, congregations, communities, and the nation can help every child have that start. Have them record their ideas on flip chart paper. After 10 minutes, reconvene the group and have each small group report on their ideas.

Decide if there are one or more ideas that the group would like to pursue putting into action.

Campaigning for the Children: Looking for Leaders to Care for All Children

Remind participants that this is an election year. While it is inappropriate (and illegal!) for congregations to engage in partisan politics (working for or against a particular candidate or political party), it is entirely appropriate for congregations and members to consider what concerns their faith calls them to stand up for, and what kind of leadership embodies the principles of justice and compassion.

Ask each participant to think about what a candidate for political office ought to stand for that would treat all children as good and valuable and help care for them. If a legislator is serious about public *service*, what commitments should we expect them to make for children's well-being?

Ask each participant to write five priorities political leaders should have in order to treat all children as good and help care for them as part of God's good creation. When they are done writing, invite them to share their priorities aloud. This should not be seen as a time for debate. Each person's priorities, like the vote she or he casts, are a personal decision for them to make, hopefully illumined by the information presented and discussion they have engaged in.

4. Closing

Invite participants to join in the responsive celebration of children drawn from a Brit Milah ceremony.

CELEBRATION OF CHILDREN

(From a Brit Milah ceremony.)

Leader: In every birth,
People: Blessed is the wonder.

Leader: In every creation,
People: Blessed is new being.

Leader: In every child,
People: Blessed is life.

Leader: In every hope,
People: Blessed is the potential.

Leader: In every transition,
People: Blessed is the beginning.

Leader: In every existence,
People: Blessed are the possibilities.

Leader: In every love,
People: Blessed are the tears.

Leader: In every life,
People: Blessed is the love.

**Unison: And in our lives, blessed are
our children and the renewal and fulfillment
given to our families, congregations, community,
and world.**

CHILDREN TODAY ARE BEING LEFT BEHIND

(All of the following stories are true. The names marked by an asterisk have been changed to protect the privacy of those involved.)

Children Need a Healthy Start

When Bobby*, a preschooler from a New England city, scratched a mosquito bite on his leg, the area became infected. His parents took him to a doctor, who prescribed an antibiotic. But because Bobby's father earned very low wages at his job, the family could not immediately afford to buy the prescription.

As a result of the family's poverty, the infection grew dangerously out of control, and Bobby was hospitalized for three days in order to receive intravenous antibiotics. Doctors estimated that each of those hospital days cost about $800.

Children Need a Head Start

Until recently, Bernadette Monteleone and Charles Lampkin's child care expenses were so high that they constantly worried about how to buy food or pay the rent on time. Preschool costs for both Charles Edward, 3, and Chelsea, 5, ran $100 a week. Together, the couple earns under $20,000 a year, not enough to afford such high child care payments. In February 1998, however, Bernadette received word that the state child care assistance she'd applied for months before came through. This help is now saving the family roughly $60 a week.

"Before we received the subsidy, it was very difficult, and a lot of times we came up short," Bernadette says. "It gives us a little extra money to put toward bills—rent, utilities, and bus passes—and to help buy food and clothes for the children."

Toby Simon, on the other hand, is one of the many parents in America who earn too much to qualify for state assistance, but too little to afford full-time child care. Last September Toby, who earns $35,000 a year, made arrangements for her daughter Hattie, nearly 2, with a family child care provider. She explained that she doesn't have much money, and the provider agreed to give Toby a price break, charging her $200 a week instead of $275.

After a few months, though, the provider informed Toby that Hattie would have to leave. She was told that parents who could afford to pay full price for care were clamoring for space with the provider, who desperately needed the extra money. Now Toby is searching for an alternative arrangement that she can afford.

"Hattie had been really happy there, and I thought she was doing very well," says Toby. "I was just completely devastated by this."

The Monteleone-Lampkins and the Simons are just two of the millions of working families in the United States who are struggling to find and keep quality, affordable child care. Bernadette and Charles's story has a happy ending, but for parents like Toby and many others, there seems to be no relief in sight.

Children Need a Fair Start

Sally* and her husband have been separated from their children for more than three months because they cannot find a place to live. After they lost their apartment because they could not afford the rent increase, the family lived in their car until the weather turned cold. Then, in desperation, the father secretly sheltered his children during the night in the warehouse where he worked, stopping when he feared that he would lose his job if discovered. Without a place to live, the parents finally put their children in the temporary care of the state

(continued on page 105)

(continued from page 104)

welfare division, which placed them in separate foster homes. The children, still apart, are having increasing problems in school, and their parents have been unable to find an affordable apartment that will accept the whole family.

Children Need a Safe Start

"Hi. My name is Bakari Clay and I'm going to tell you all about my neighborhood. The neighborhood I live in wasn't bad until about a year ago. It used to be safe and clean until they started to sell drugs and do drive-bys and stick people up. I think that people are so dumb for killing each other over drugs, coats, shoes, chains, and other material items. Some days I'm scared to even walk to school by myself thinking I'm gonna get killed....

But I just take a deep breath and keep my head to the sky, hoping that the police or someone can make my neighborhood safe to live in again someday. There's trouble anywhere you go so I'm gonna do all I can to help my neighborhood be the cleanest and safest place I can but I'm only eight years old—I can't do it all by myself." (From *My Neighborhood: The Words and Pictures of Inner-City Children*, compilation and narrative by Linda Waldman, 1993, Hyde Park Bank Foundation, Chicago.)

Children Need a Moral Start

High school senior Miguel DeJesus of New Britain, Conn., had a lot going for him. He was enrolled in a college preparatory course. Both of his parents had jobs. He and his mother were involved in their Baptist church. But Miguel wrote this in a youth literary magazine about the children of his generation:

> "The innocence is gone. Never again will kids be able to go outside and not be exposed to drugs, hunger, or poverty. The youth of today have nothing to do. They have no place to go. Especially here in New Britain, it's dead out here. We don't even have a movie theater. Then you wonder why we have so many gangs out here. If you have nowhere to go and nothing to do you feel alone, and when you feel alone you need to belong to something. When we have nothing to do, some of us turn to drugs and alcohol. The end of innocence is here.... The [kids] don't know the academics, but they know the streets, and they think that's all they need to know."

On November 8, 1993, three months after writing this, Miguel was shot and killed on the steps of his high school.

Unless otherwise noted, all stories were previously published in CDF Reports.

LEAVE NO CHILD BEHIND

No child should be left behind. Every child needs and deserves a Healthy Start, a Head Start, a Fair Start, a Safe Start, and a Moral Start in life.

A Healthy Start means that children have healthy bodies and minds, and are assured a comprehensive health and mental health system that provides preventive care when they are well and treatment when they are ill.

A Head Start means that children have strong parents from birth who are supported by communities that truly value families, get the early childhood foundation they need to get ready for school, and attend high quality schools that inspire, respect, and support every child's success.

A Fair Start means that children grow up in families with jobs that pay livable wages and are protected from poverty, hunger, and homelessness when parents cannot adequately provide.

A Safe Start means that children are safe and secure in their homes, neighborhoods, and schools, are protected from the guns that kill a child every two hours, and have safe havens before and after school and during summer months.

A Moral Start means that parents, other caring adults, and congregations recognize and communicate every child's sacred worth and guide children by example in developing positive, enduring values of justice, compassion, and respect for self and others. Children of all ages need loving limits, discipline, and attention to successfully navigate the paths to adulthood.

Interfaith Worship Resources

This section provides suggestions for planning an interfaith Children's Sabbath, a sample interfaith service, and a sample reflection for an interfaith service. It also includes readings and prayers from a variety of faith traditions. These can be used in an interfaith celebration, to enrich your congregation's own Children's Sabbath and broaden its understanding of other faith traditions, or to spark Children's Sabbath planning for congregations of those faith traditions.

Planning an Interfaith Celebration

Organizing a community-wide interfaith service may sound like a daunting task, but it can be done successfully, and can be a tremendous contribution to a community. These are suggested ways to coordinate the event. Feel free to adapt this process to suit your needs.

1. Build a team. Connect with two, three, four, or more people to help you get started. Then convene an advisory committee of eight to fifteen members. Strive to build an advisory committee that represents the full range of religious bodies, races, and ethnicities of your community.

2. Get the ball rolling. Develop an efficient agenda for the initial meeting of the advisory committee. A productive meeting will generate energy, enthusiasm, and continued commitment. Key items to determine include the date, site, range of events, and point people to assume responsibility for aspects of the event. You may find it helpful to show the video *National Observance of Children's Sabbaths: Raising Voices, Linking Hands for Children* to convey the purpose and power of the Children's Sabbath (see Order Form at back for ordering information).

3. Recruit others. Begin to contact as many congregations and community organizations as you can to get them on board. Be sure to invite congregations of all ethnic and racial groups. Network with ministerial, rabbinical, and interfaith associations, schools, social clubs, and organizations dealing with children, poverty, violence, health, hunger, homelessness, education, and parenting. Contact them by letter and include a response form for those who wish to participate. Follow up with a phone call. Make a contact list of affirmative responses that you can add to later.

4. Develop a game plan and assign areas for coordination. Areas to coordinate include site selection, administration and funding, worship planning, music, outreach/promotion/media, and activities that will raise awareness of children's concerns and generate service and advocacy.

5. Schedule the interfaith service for a time that does not exclude any group's participation. For example, scheduling an interfaith service on Saturday afternoon, during the Jewish Shabbat, would prevent some Jews from attending. Sunday morning scheduling is likely to conflict with most church services. Sunday afternoon or evening is usually the best time for an interfaith event.

Be aware, however, that you will need to do lots of outreach and promotion to generate strong attendance for an interfaith service, whenever it is scheduled. See the promotion suggestions in Section 2.

6. Find a suitable site. Seek advice from people who have done similar events, and choose a site as early as possible. Feasible sites for interfaith activities include auditoriums, hospitals, convention centers, atriums of public buildings, and schools. Of course, religious places of worship are also good sites. If you use a congregation's building, be sure the religious leader is involved in the planning, since he or she will know the logistics of the site.

Some things to consider in selecting a site:
Size: Make sure it is large enough to accommodate the crowd you expect, but not so large as to look empty.
Staging: Will it accommodate choirs and a procession? Is there a good sound and lighting system?

Location: Is it centrally located and convenient for all segments of the community?
Cost: Try to find a site that will host the service without any charge.
Worship space: Is it conducive to interfaith worship? Will it foster unity among persons who don't know each other? Consider temporary removal of symbols or objects that might cause others distress (if possible). Also, consider the addition of banners and symbols or expressions of welcome that may make guests feel more at home.
Parking: Is parking available or is public transportation nearby?
Accessibility: Is it accessible to people with disabilities? (Remember to have an interpreter for those who are deaf or hearing impaired.)

Liturgical Suggestions for Interfaith Services

If *everyone* will be speaking or singing it, be sure it is inclusive. If a part of the interfaith service, such as a prayer or song, will be spoken or sung by the congregation, be sure that it does not include language that feels exclusive (such as "Jesus Christ" or "Muhammad"). Instead, draw on the universal and unifying aspects of our various religious traditions. For songs that everyone will be invited to join in, keeping the references primarily to "God" is the safest bet. Other appropriate ways of addressing God in an interfaith service are Creator, Source of All Life, Our God and Sustainer, Eternal Creator, and Source of Our Being. Some appropriate closing addresses include "in Thy name we pray," "in the name of God," or simply, "Amen."

Have representatives present readings or prayers specific to their traditions. If individual leaders will be presenting readings or offering prayers, they may include references specific to their own traditions (such as "Jesus Christ" or "Muhammad"). Similarly, a choir that is performing an anthem could sing music specific to its tradition. Just make sure that you invite representatives from a range of faith traditions, and encourage them to select readings and prayers that are as inclusive as possible and do not denigrate other religious traditions. (If you won't have time to include readings from every religious tradition represented, you may want to print additional readings in the service program.)

Be as broadly representative as possible. Try to include representatives from as many faith traditions as possible. Also be sure to balance gender, racial, and ethnic representation. You may not be able to give every representative a "speaking part" in the service. Invite those who will not be able to speak in the service to participate in an opening procession (with each processor wearing robes or other religious garb appropriate to their tradition) and sit in a special section, either on the stage with the speakers or at the front of the congregation. List the processors and their religious affiliation in the service program.

Know ahead of time what will be spoken and sung. An interfaith service is not the right time for surprises! It is important that the service have a unified message that lifts up children's needs and inspires people to action. One would never constrain leaders from reading or praying what they feel is right in services entirely under their leadership, but in a cooperative service like an interfaith Children's Sabbath that aims to lift up particular concerns, it is entirely appropriate to exercise such oversight.

• One possibility is to use a service that you and your planning team write in advance. Assign the pre-written parts to religious leaders. The only part that would not be pre-written would be the reflection. It is important to select a leader to give the reflection who you are confident will speak in terms appropriate for an interfaith gathering and will address the children's concerns that are the focus of the service. The sample interfaith Children's Sabbath service in this section is one model that you could use. For a guide to additional sermon resources in this manual, turn to page 40.

- Another possibility is to have the invited religious leaders write their own "parts" or select their own readings. In this case, be sure that they give you copies of their prayers or readings in advance. If any prayer or reading is not in keeping with the Children's Sabbath theme, give that leader more guidance about the Children's Sabbath theme and purpose and ask her or him to select another prayer or reading.

Be clear about timing. An interfaith service that strives to be representative runs the risk of being too long. A sense of time and appropriate length for services also varies by faith tradition. When you invite leaders, be sure they know how much time has been allotted for their part. Emphasize that everyone must keep to their allotted time. (This is another reason for having advance copies of what each leader will be reading or praying.) Know ahead of time what you will do if the service begins to run too long and you need to shorten it. The least offensive place to cut is usually verses from a congregational song, or an entire song. Be sure that the music director knows in advance that this is a possibility, and decide who will make the decision and who will communicate it to the leaders and congregation, if necessary.

Brief the leadership in advance. Ask all of the participating religious leaders (both those with speaking parts and those who will be processing) to gather 30-60 minutes before the start of the service. At that time, give each a copy of the service program, allow time for them to robe or put on their religious garb, and brief them on the logistics of the service: who will process with whom, where they will sit, which podium they will speak from, and other such details. You may want to designate one leader to be responsible for filling in if a leader doesn't show up or handling other unexpected occurrences.

Convene a special combined choir for the service. Invite a wide range of congregations' choirs to participate (children's, adults, or both). Then send the selected music to each choir director, who will teach the song to her or his choir during their own rehearsals. Schedule several combined rehearsals during which all of the choirs will sing together, under the direction of one appointed director. Incidentally, this is a good way to build attendance, since many proud family members are likely to attend to hear their children sing.

Interfaith Children's Sabbath Service

Joining Hearts, Hands, and Voices to Leave No Child Behind

Gathering Words

(Said by one person, or by leaders of different faith traditions. If led by different leaders, have them read the last line in unison. You may want to have representatives of each faith present—adults or children—bring forward banners or other symbols of their faith tradition. Be sure you know in advance what these will be.)

Come you who worship Adonai.
Come you who worship Allah.
Come you who worship the triune God, Father, Son, and Holy Spirit.
Come you who worship Buddha, Bahaullah, Mother Earth, Source and Light,
Come all who worship the Eternal.
By whatever name we know God,
let us affirm together God's calling to serve and protect the children entrusted to our care.
Let us celebrate our common calling and worship God together this day.

Hymn: "Immortal, Invisible, God Only Wise"

Opening Prayer

Eternal God, we bring to this place many hearts, hands, and voices. We come with many concerns for children in need today, and we come with gratitude for the gifts of children. We come from different traditions, yet each prompts us to care for children, inspires us to reach out to them, and sustains us when this calling is challenging. Use us this day and every day, we pray. Join our hearts and hands and voices in answering your call to serve your children. Amen.

Anthem

Words From Many Faiths

(Intersperse with music. See Resources From Many Faiths at the end of this service for examples of readings and prayers from a variety of faith traditions. Christian and Jewish resources are in Sections 3 and 4 respectively. Use some of these, or invite your leaders to select and write their own.)

Reflection

(This may be a time for a speaker to offer a message to the congregation. As noted in Liturgical Suggestions, be sure that the speaker is prepared to appropriately address an interfaith gathering and is advised about the time allotted for this portion of the service. Five minutes—obviously less than a traditional sermon—may be appropriate. See the Sample Interfaith Reflection for an example.)

Hymn: "Here I Am, Lord"

Prayers of the People

Leader: Let us turn to God in prayer.
For babies born too soon and too small, for sick and injured children without health care, for parents who bear the double pain of a sick child and inability to afford care,
People: God, grant them a Healthy Start.

Leader: For children whose bright promise is squelched in poor quality child care, for children denied the opportunity of Head Start, for children and youths whose schools may teach failure and discouragement,
People: God, grant them a Head Start.

Leader: For children bearing the brunt of poverty, with hungry tummies and heavy hearts, for parents who work hard at jobs that still leave them below poverty and unable to provide their families' basic needs,
People: God, grant them a Fair Start.

Leader: For children who cower under beds and clutch safety blankets, fearing bullets outside their windows or beatings inside their homes, for youths whose fear, despair, and anger lead them to carry guns and plan their funerals, for parents who see their children slipping into trouble and don't know what to do,
People: God, grant them a Safe Start.

Leader: For children who don't know their inherent, God-given worth, for youths abandoned to find their own values who turn to peers and media to measure self-worth, for parents who long to guide their children but wonder if it is too late,
People: God, grant them a Moral Start.

Leader: With God, it is never too late for us. God offers us fresh beginnings every day, the chance to find the new start we need, the opportunity to provide a new start for a child. Thanks be to God. Amen.

Anthem

Charge to the Congregation

(Invite a dynamic speaker to present a charge to the congregation. Be very clear about the time allotted for this portion. Five to ten minutes may be appropriate.)

Act of Commitment

Leader: God calls us, not just this day but every day, to nurture and protect children whom God has entrusted to our care. God has given each of us gifts and skills to use for the well-being of children.

Let each of us commit to reaching out and caring for children in the way God calls us, whether it is to wipe a tear, bandage a scraped knee, comfort a scraped heart, tutor a struggling student, paint over graffiti, plant a community garden, become a foster parent, provide an internship, coach a sports team, or hold a hand.

People (sing):
Take my life, and let it be consecrated, God, to thee.
Take my moments and my days; let them flow in ceaseless praise.
Take my hands, and let them move at the impulse of thy love.
Take my feet, and let them be swift and beautiful for thee.

Leader: Our God calls us to do justice, and to speak out for those who cannot speak. Let us commit to be voices for justice, proclaiming God's concern for those who are young, weak, and poor. Let us find ways to support children's causes with our time, talents, and treasure.

People (sing):
Take my voice, and let me laud always, only, you my God.
Take my lips, and let them be filled with messages from thee.
Take my silver and my gold; not a mite would I withhold.
Take my intellect, and use every power as thou shalt choose.

Leader: As we serve and speak out for children, may we be guided and sustained by the one who came to us as servant and advocate. Let us rely on prayer and the believing community to keep our vision faithful, our hearts loving, and our commitment steady.

People (sing):
Take my will, and make it thine; it shall be no longer mine.
Take my heart, it is thine own; it shall be thy royal throne.
Take my love, my God, I pour at thy feet its treasure-store.
Take myself, and I will be ever, only, all for thee.

Hymn: (Cuban) "I Am Sent by God"

Sending Forth

(Please hold the hands of the people next to you.)

These are the hands God has given us to work
in God's world:
comforting hands to hold
tender hands to bandage
generous hands to give
strong hands to protect
guiding hands to teach
faithful hands to pray
Look at your hands; see the gifts and the possibilities
Look at your neighbors' hands; see the strength and the partnership
We have many hands and one calling. Let us go forth to serve all children.

Take My Life, and Let It Be

1. Take my life, and let it be con-se-cra-ted,
2. Take my voice, and let me laud al-ways, on-ly,
3. Take my will, and make it thine; it shall be no

God, to thee. Take my mo-ments and my days;
for my God. Take my lips, and let them be
long-er mine. Take my heart, it is thine own;

let them flow in cease-less praise. Take my hands, and
filled with mes-sag-es from thee. Take my sil-ver
it shall be thy roy-al throne. Take my love, my

let them move at the im-pulse of thy love.
and my gold; not a mite would I with-hold.
God, I pour at thy feet its trea-sure-store.

Take my feet, and let them be swift and beau-ti-ful for thee.
Take my in-tel-lect, and use ev-ery power as thou shalt choose.
Take my-self, and I will be ev-er, on-ly, all for thee.

WORDS: Adapted from Frances R. Havergal, 1873 (Rom. 12:1)
MUSIC: Louis J. F. Herold, 1839, arr. by George Kingley, 1839   77.77D

MESSIAH

I Am Sent by God

Words traditional Cuban, translation by Donald Schmidt Music traditional Cuban, arr. by Alan Whitmore
Copyright © Wood Lake Books. Used by permission.

SAMPLE INTERFAITH REFLECTION
"HOW ARE THE CHILDREN?"

By the Rev. Pat Hoertdoerfer, Unitarian Universalist Association, Boston, Mass.
(based on a sermon by the Rev. Dr. Patrick T. O'Neill, Senior Minister,
First Unitarian Association, Wilmington, Del.)

Among the most accomplished and fabled ethnic groups of Africa, no group was considered to have warriors more fearsome or more intelligent than the mighty Masai. It is perhaps surprising then to learn the traditional greeting that passed between Masai warriors. *"Kasserian Ingera,"* one would always say to another. It means, "And how are the children?"

It is still the traditional greeting among the Masai, acknowledging the high value that the Masai always place on their children's well-being. Even warriors with no children of their own would always give the traditional answer, "All the children are well." Meaning, of course, that peace and safety prevail, that the priorities of protecting the young, the powerless, are in place, that Masai society has not forgotten its reason for being, its proper functions and responsibilities. "All the children are well" means that life is good. It means that the daily struggles of existence do not preclude proper caring for their young.

I wonder how it might affect our consciousness of our own children's welfare if in our cultures we took to greeting each other with this daily question: "And how are the children?" If we heard that question and passed it along to each other a dozen times a day, I wonder if it would begin to make a difference in the reality of how children are thought of or cared for in our own country?

If every adult among us, parent and non-parent alike, felt an equal weight for the daily care and protection of all the children in our community, in our town, in our state, in our country, I wonder if we could truly say without hesitation, "The children are well, yes, all the children are well"?

What would it be like if religious leaders began every worship service by answering the question, "And how are the children?" If the teacher began every class by answering the question, "And how are the children?" If every town leader had to answer the same question at the beginning of every meeting: "And how are the children? Are they well?" If every business leader and corporate executive had to answer the same question at the beginning of every work day: "And how are the children? Are they all well?" Wouldn't it be interesting to hear their answers? What would it be like? I wonder...I wonder...

Let's begin here and greet families and friends in this gathered community with "And how are the children?" And before we can respond to one another, "All the children are well," what actions must we take in our community? In our town? In our state?

And how are the children? Working together, may all our children be well.

Resources From Many Faiths

The following pages provide resources from a variety of faith traditions: the Baha'i faith, Buddhism, Hinduism, Islam, Native American traditions, Sikhism, and Unitarian Universalism. The resources include passages from sacred texts or other writings central to these traditions, prayers, and reflections. For Christian and Jewish resources, please draw from the extensive materials provided elsewhere in this book.

These resources may be used in an interfaith Children's Sabbath service, to spark a Children's Sabbath in congregations of these traditions, or to enrich the Children's Sabbath of congregations from other traditions. They also may be used in an interfaith educational program you develop for your Children's Sabbath.

 ## The Baha'i Faith

Readings

Strive that your actions day by day may be beautiful prayers.

('Abdu'l-Baha)

Let your heart burn with loving kindness for all who may cross your path.

('Abdu'l-Baha)

Service to the world of humanity should be obligatory. Every student should know, with perfect certainty, that he is the brother of the people of all religions and nations and that he should be without religious, racial, national, patriotic or political bias, so that he may find the thoughts of universal peace and the love of humankind firmly established in his heart. He should know himself as a servant of human society of all the countries in the world. He should see God as the Heavenly Father and all the servants as his children, counting all of the nations, parties, and sects as one family. The mothers in the homes, the teachers in the schools, the professors in the universities, and the leaders in the lofty gatherings, must cause these thoughts to be penetrative and effective, as the spirit circulating in the veins and nerves of the children and pupils, so that the world of humanity may be delivered from the calamities of fanaticism, war, battle, hate and obstinacy, and so that the nether world may become the paradise of heaven.

('Abdu'l-Baha)

Prayers

O Lord! Make this youth radiant, and confer Thy bounty upon this poor creature. Bestow upon him knowledge, grant him added strength at the break of every morn and guard him within the shelter of Thy protection so that he may be freed from error, may devote himself to the service of Thy Cause, may guide the wayward, lead the hapless, free the captives and awaken the heedless, that all may be blessed with thy remembrance and praise. Thou art the Mighty and the Powerful.

('Abdu'l-Baha)

O my God! O my God! Unite the hearts of Thy servants, and reveal to them Thy great purpose. May they follow Thy commandments and abide in Thy law. Help them, O God, in their endeavor, and grant them strength to serve Thee. O God! Leave them not to themselves, but guide their steps by the light of Thy knowledge, and cheer their hearts by Thy love. Verily, Thou art their Helper and their Lord.

(Baha'u'llah)

Buddhism

Readings

Many people seem to be excited about the new millennium, but the new millennium in itself will be nothing special. As we enter into the new millennium things will be the same; there will be nothing unusual. However, if we really want the next millennium to be happier, more peaceful, and more harmonious for humankind, we will have to make the effort to make it so. This is in our hands, but especially in the hands of the younger generation....

If we are going to make the right kind of efforts to make the future of the world better, I believe the following matters are of importance.

1. While engaging in material progress and taking care of physical well-being, we need to pay equal attention to developing peace of mind, and thus taking care of the internal aspect of our being.

2. Along with education, which generally deals only with academic accomplishments, we need to develop more altruism and a sense of caring and responsibility for others in the minds of the younger generation studying in various educational institutions....

3. This past century in some ways has been a century of war and bloodshed. It has seen a year-by-year increase in defense spending by most countries in the world. If we are to change this trend we must seriously consider the concept of nonviolence, which is a physical expression of compassion. In order to make nonviolence a reality, we must first work on internal disarmament, and then proceed to work on external disarmament. By internal disarmament, I mean ridding ourselves of all the negative emotions that result in violence. External disarmament will also have to be done gradually, step by step....

4. We need to address the issue of the gap between the rich and the poor, both globally and nationally. This inequality, with some sections of the human community having abundance, and others on the same planet going hungry or even dying of starvation, is not only morally wrong, but practically also a source of problems....

We need to seriously look into these matters that concern us all if we are to look forward to the future with some hope.

(Excerpts from a message from His Holiness The XIVth Dalai Lama of Tibet, Tenzin Gyatso, January 1, 2000)

It is time for elders to listen to the child's voice. You see, in the child's mind there is no demarcation of different nations, no demarcation of different social systems of ideology. Children know in their minds that all children are the same, all human beings are the same. So, from that viewpoint, their minds are more unbiased. When people get older, though, they start to say, "our nation," "our religion," "our system." Once that demarcation occurs, then people don't bother much about what happens to others. It's easier to introduce social responsibility into a child's mind.

(His Holiness the XIVth Dalai Lama of Tibet, Tenzin Gyatso, in *My Tibet*, written with Galen Rowell, excerpted in *A Sourcebook for Earth's Community of Religions* [1995])

Prayer

May every creature abound in well-being and peace.
May every living being, weak or strong, the long and the small,
the short and the medium-sized, the mean and the great—
May every living being, seen or unseen, those dwelling far off, those near by,
those already born, those waiting to be born—
May all attain inward peace.

Let no one deceive one another. Let no one despise another in any situation.
Let no one, from antipathy or hatred, wish evil to anyone at all.
Just as a mother, with her own life, protects her only son from hurt,
So within yourself foster a limitless concern for every living creature.
Display a heart of boundless love for all the world
In all its height and depth and broad extent—
Love unrestrained, without hate or enmity.
Then as you stand or walk, sit or lie, until overcome by drowsiness,
Devote your mind entirely to this, it is known as living here the life divine.

(From *A Sourcebook for Earth's Community of Religions* [1995])

Hinduism

**Prepared by Dr. Siva Subrahmanian,
United Hindu Jain Temples, Potomac, Md.,
Vice-President, Interfaith Conference of
Metropolitan Washington, Washington, D.C.**

Benediction in Vedic Sanskrit
Pasyati Puthram, Pasyati Poutram
Aputraahas santu putrinaha, Putrinas santhu poutrinaha
Daanyam, dhanam, Bahuputralaabham.

May one live to see children, May one live to see
grandchildren,
May those that are childless have children,
May those that have children have grandchildren!
May you have lots of grain, wealth, and many children.

Aphorisms in Ancient Tamil
Kuzhal Inidu Yaazh Inidhu Enbar tham makkal
Mazhalai chchol kelaadhavar.

They say the flute is sweet to hear or the lyre is sweet.
It is only because they did not hear the lisping words of
their children.

Thandhai maharkku aartrum nandri avaiyaththu
Mundri iruppaccheyal.

The great help a father can render to his child is to
raise him to be the best in the world.

Eenra pozhudir periduvakkun than maganai
Chaanron enakketta thaai.

Mother is happy when she bears a child, but much happier
when that child is hailed as a great person.

Song in Modern Tamil
Un kannil neer vazhindai, en nenjil udhiram kottudhadee,
en kannin paavai anro, en uyir ninnadandro.

If I see tears falling from your eyes (dear child),
my heart bleeds,
Oh darling of my eye! My life is yours (I live only for you).

(Bala Krishnan and Siva Subramanian)

Islamic

Reading from the Holy Qur'an:

It is not righteousness
That ye turn your faces
Towards East or West;
But it is righteousness—
To believe in Allah
And the Last Day,
And the Angels,
And the Book,
And the Messengers;
To spend of your substance,
Out of love for Him,
For your kin,
For orphans,
For the needy,
For the wayfarer,
For those who ask,
And for the ransom of slaves;
To be steadfast in prayer,
And give Zakat,
To fulfil the contracts
Which ye have made;
And to be firm and patient,
In pain (or suffering)
And adversity,
And throughout
All periods of panic.
Such are the people
Of truth, the God-fearing.

(Surah 2A.177)

﴿ لَّيْسَ ٱلْبِرَّ أَن تُوَلُّوا۟ وُجُوهَكُمْ قِبَلَ ٱلْمَشْرِقِ
وَٱلْمَغْرِبِ وَلَٰكِنَّ ٱلْبِرَّ مَنْ ءَامَنَ بِٱللَّهِ وَٱلْيَوْمِ
ٱلْءَاخِرِ وَٱلْمَلَٰٓئِكَةِ وَٱلْكِتَٰبِ وَٱلنَّبِيِّۦنَ
وَءَاتَى ٱلْمَالَ عَلَىٰ حُبِّهِۦ ذَوِى ٱلْقُرْبَىٰ
وَٱلْيَتَٰمَىٰ وَٱلْمَسَٰكِينَ وَٱبْنَ ٱلسَّبِيلِ
وَٱلسَّآئِلِينَ وَفِى ٱلرِّقَابِ وَأَقَامَ ٱلصَّلَوٰةَ
وَءَاتَى ٱلزَّكَوٰةَ وَٱلْمُوفُونَ بِعَهْدِهِمْ إِذَا
عَٰهَدُوا۟ وَٱلصَّٰبِرِينَ فِى ٱلْبَأْسَآءِ وَٱلضَّرَّآءِ وَحِينَ
ٱلْبَأْسِ أُو۟لَٰٓئِكَ ٱلَّذِينَ صَدَقُوا۟ وَأُو۟لَٰٓئِكَ هُمُ
ٱلْمُتَّقُونَ ﴿١٧٧﴾

Prayers

O Allah! You are our Creator. You are our provider and sustainer. All things are in Your hands and all authority rests with You and You alone. You have no helpers and need no assistance. Without Your guidance and light, we are in darkness. Help us. Without Your help, we are helpless. We depend solely on You.

O Allah! You know that the children are our future, and we have not done what you have commanded us to do. Have mercy on us and overlook our faults. Protect the children, Allah, for surely you are the only protector. Give us the wisdom and the strength to work together for the welfare of all of our beloved children. O Allah! Save the children.

(Prayers prepared by Amir Al-Islam,
The Muslim Center for Civilizational Dialogue, New York, N.Y.)

Native American Traditions

Readings

It is strictly believed and understood by the Sioux that a child is the greatest gift from Wakan Tanka ("Great Spirit"), in response to many devout prayers, sacrifices, and promises. Therefore the child is considered "sent by Wakan Tanka," through some element—namely the element of human nature.

(Robert Higheagle, Teton Sioux, in *Native American Wisdom*, Running Press, 1994)

In our way of life...with every decision we make, we always keep in mind the Seventh Generation of children to come....When we walk upon Mother Earth, we always plant our feet carefully, because we know that the faces of future generations are looking up at us from beneath the ground. We never forget them.

(Oren Lyons, Faithkeeper, Onondaga Nation, Earth Day 1993 Pledge)

Sioux Prayer

Great Spirit, Great Spirit, my Grandfather,
all over the earth the faces of living things are alike...
Look upon these faces of children without number and
with children in their arms,
that they may face the winds and walk the good road to the
day of quiet.

(Black Elk [1863-1950], Oglala Sioux holy man)

Ojibway Prayer

Grandfather,
Look at our brokenness.
We know that in all Creation
Only the human family
Has strayed from the Sacred Way.

We know that we are the ones
Who are divided
And we are the ones
Who must come back together
To walk in the Sacred Way.

Grandfather,
Sacred One,
Teach us love, compassion, honor
That we may heal the earth
And heal each other.

Sikhism

**Prepared by Amrit Kaur,
Guru Gobind Singh Foundation,
Washington, D.C.**

The following hymns have been selected from the Sikh Scripture Shri Guru Granth Sahib. It is a large volume of 1430 pages that is a repository of Sikh philosophy, religion, and at times political and social commentary on the existing conditions. The Sikh Gurus (Divine Masters) had the firm belief that life cannot be lived in isolation. A true devotee of God lives a life with responsibilities toward family, and society, and with constant awareness of the Infinite within.

God makes me do what He wills: For I am unwise and
ignorant
I, your child, seek refuge, O God: And You will save
my honor
O my Supreme Lord, You are my Father and Mother
For, in Your Mercy, You sustain me, and I do what is
in Your Will.
You uphold Your children, O God: And the leading string
is in Your Hands
That what is in Your Will, I do: And I seek Your refuge
for ever.

This hymn is inscribed on page 496 of Guru Granth Sahib. It has been composed by the fifth Guru (holy preceptor) Arjun Dev as a blessing to children:

Oh Child! This is your mother's blessing. May you never forget the God even for a moment and always remember the Lord of Universe. By meditating on Him all the sins are obliterated and generations are enlightened. Ponder over always on that Lord who is boundless. May the true Guru be kind to you and may you nurture love for the company of saints. May the preservation of your honor by the Lord be our attire: Singing of His praise your daily bread; Drink ever the nectar of God's name and live long; By remembering God may you attain the bliss. May joys and playful pleasures be yours. May your hopes be realized and may you never get distressed. Let your mind hover like a humming black bumblebee* at the lotus feet of God. Says the humble Nanak,** be attached to God like a pied-cuckoo that rejoices in ecstasy on finding raindrop.*

*Bumblebee hovering over lotus and pied-cuckoo yearning for raindrop are symbolic of everlasting love in Indian folk lore.

**There are ten Gurus in Sikhism and they all refer to themselves as Nanak, signifying the continuation of the same divine light that first manifested in Guru Nanak, the founder of Sikhism.

Unitarian Universalism

**Prepared by Pat Hoertdoerfer, Unitarian
Universalist Association, Boston, Mass.**

Prayer

May we never rest until every child of earth in every
generation
is free from all prisons of the mind, and of the body, and of
the spirit,
until the earth and the hills and the seas shall dance
and the universe itself resounds with the joyful cry,
"Behold! I am!"

(By the Reverend John Cummins)

Responsive Reading: We Look to the Children

We look to the children: and for the children, we dream of
their tomorrows.

Let this be our dream for the children:
That they may know, in the brief years of their childhood,
the warmth of our love—since only thus can they learn
to love.

Let this be our dream for the children:
That they may always be fully respected as persons—
since only thus can they gain self-respect and learn respect
for others.

Let this be our dream for the children:
That they may find us, their elders, seeking to preserve and
to create things of beauty—since only thus can they learn
to appreciate the beautiful and live creatively.

Let this be our dream for the children:
That day by day they may find themselves more and more
free to make their own mistakes and learn from them; to
discover their own meanings and grow by them; to improve
our ways and adopt their own and mature by them—since
only thus can they become better persons than we have been.

Let this be our dream for the children:
That in their later years, they may honor their elders, not
through a sense of duty but with a sincere affection born of
the fact that we did not place fetters on their truest freedom
of mind and spirit and person.

**Hopefully, humbly, we dream these dreams for
the children, and may ours be the knowledge that
only through our deeds shall these dreams come
to be.**

Activity Ideas for All Faiths to Leave No Child Behind

The activities that you plan for your Children's Sabbath day or weekend can be a highlight of the experience. When the worship service raises awareness of children's needs and underscores the faith imperative for responding, people are eager to get into action right away!

As you plan activities for the Children's Sabbath, keep the following tips in mind:

First, offer a range of activities focusing on raising awareness, hands-on service, and advocacy. Making a difference for children requires all three kinds of effort! It also enables people to choose activities based on their particular skills and interests. (We've marked the activities with symbols to guide your selection: An ear/eye=raise awareness, a hand=hands-on service, and a mouth=advocacy.)

Second, plan some activities that can be completed on the Children's Sabbath (such as making sandwiches for a shelter serving families) **and some that will lead people into long-term commitments** (such as signing up volunteers to help at the shelter once a month).

Third, plan activities that will engage all ages. For example, if there is a table to write letters to elected officials, provide crayons and markers so that young children can draw pictures to enclose, or have them dictate their letters to an older child or adult.

Fourth, use the Children's Sabbath to reinforce existing congregational programs that serve children while introducing new opportunities to serve children and families. For example, highlight accomplishments, recruit new people to help, or solicit donations.

Finally, be sure you are prepared to guide people in the activities so that they understand the connection between the worship and the action. You may want to provide a preview of the activities on a bulletin insert or during the announcement time in worship. During the activity period, it works best to have several people at each activity who are prepared to explain and guide participation.

Conduct a Site Visit to See the Challenges and Solutions First-Hand

Arrange a tour to raise awareness of children's needs and solutions (on the Children's Sabbath weekend or the following week). Have people sign up in advance to participate. For example, arrange visits to a neonatal intensive care unit, a Head Start program, a shelter or soup kitchen serving families, a juvenile detention facility, and a congregational program (your own or another's) for children. For each site, have the host provide a briefing about the people they serve, the kinds of need they see, the causes and the solutions. Have them discuss how people can work for positive solutions to prevent or address the needs. Where possible and appropriate, provide participants with the opportunity to talk with the people being served, not just those who staff the programs. End with a debriefing that helps participants process what they've seen and heard and identify ways that they will respond. For more information on organizing a site visit, contact CDF's Child Watch Division at (202) 662-3588.

Map Out Resources: Develop a Chart of Available Services

Help congregation members understand what services for families are available in your community, and which are in short supply. Develop a chart or map that shows what services are available, such as child care centers, Head Start programs, health clinics, doctors' offices, hospitals, WIC sites, welfare and employment services, food banks and soup kitchens, subsidized housing, and after-school programs. Indicate how these services correspond with different income levels in your community. Where are the services located? Is there public transportation nearby? Who is eligible for the services? Is there a waiting list or are people turned away? How do or could congregations support it?

Host a "Leave No Child Behind" Community Forum

Invite a panel of speakers to address different aspects of the theme "Leave No Child Behind." Have a health care professional address a "Healthy Start"; a Head Start teacher, child care provider, professional in early childhood development, teacher, staff of an after-school program, or school administrator address a "Head Start"; a staff person from an organization serving low-income persons (such as a job training center, WIC office, emergency food and shelter services) address a "Fair Start"; a police officer, juvenile detention staff, parole officer, juvenile court judge, conflict resolution trainer, or mediator address a "Safe Start"; and a clergy person or youth group leader talk about a "Moral Start." Include a panelist who can speak about initiatives in Congress and the state legislature. Ask the speakers to describe the problems (causes and effects) and the solutions and how people can help.

In addition to hearing from professionals working in these areas, when possible and appropriate arrange to hear from the real "experts": those who are personally affected by the issue (such as parents or youths). Consider inviting legislators or candidates for public office to serve as panelists, or to respond to what the panelists present.

Invite members of the community to attend the forum in addition to your congregation's members. You may invite another area congregation to join you in sponsoring this forum. See the media tips in Section 2 for ideas about inviting the media to cover your forum.

Create a Quilt of Care

Involve congregation members in making a Quilt of Care. Provide 8"x 8" squares of fabric (light and solid colored fabrics may work best) and fabric paints or fabric markers. You could also include other scraps of cloth or felt and glue suitable for fabric. Invite each person to create a square conveying a prayer for children, a picture of children, a fact about children in need, or a symbolic commitment to leaving no child behind. After the squares have been completed, have a congregation member assemble them into a quilt. Hang it in your congregation's building as a visible reminder of children's needs and your faithful commitments.

Sponsor a Faith in Action Fair

Arrange for a variety of organizations and programs to set up tables with information about opportunities to volunteer, donate, or advocate. Include both congregational programs and community-based organizations. Encourage those staffing the tables to bring photographs or other visuals to depict their work and copies of newsletters or brochures. Urge them to be specific about volunteer needs. When possible, encourage them to offer a variety of options for ways people can support their work, including one-time help and ongoing commitments.

Give Items That Help Children Have the Start They Need

Check with organizations serving children in your community for specific needs, and consider some of the items listed below. Ask congregation members in advance to bring in some of the following items on the Children's Sabbath. (Alternatively, purchase the items with approved congregational funds.) Collect them on the Children's Sabbath, and set up a festive station for packaging the donations. Items may be wrapped with colorful paper and ribbons, tucked inside a paper bag decorated with crayons and markers, or packed into a cardboard box covered with friendly inscriptions or pictures cut from magazines. Handmade cards with a friendly line or two could be included with the packages.

- *For a Healthy Start:* assemble children's toothbrushes and children's toothpaste; first aid kit items such as adhesive bandages, children's pain reliever, thermometers, and syrup of ipecac; a paperback copy of Dr. Spock's *Baby and Child Care*; or safety items such as cabinet locks and electrical outlet guards. These could be distributed through a food pantry, shelter serving homeless families, health clinic, or other avenue. You could also collect books, puzzles, and toys for the waiting room of a community health clinic or WIC site.

- **For a Head Start:** collect children's books, puzzles and other stimulating toys, "dress-up" clothes, or puppets to give to a child care program, Head Start class, or school. Alternatively, you could make them part of a new congregational Toy Lending Library, from which family day care providers and others could borrow.

- **For a Fair Start:** collect non-perishable food items children enjoy, such as peanut butter and all-fruit jams, to donate to food banks; warm clothes such as hats, mittens, and boots to donate to shelters; or money for an emergency fund to help pay heating bills and other necessities.

- **For a Safe Start:** gather cuddly toys such as teddy bears for children going into foster care, or offer non-violent toys and games for a trade-in to get toy guns and other violence-oriented toys out of circulation.

- **For a Moral Start:** gather books and videos that promote positive values for a lending library in your congregation. Some of the books could be aimed at strengthening parenting skills while others could be written for children and youths.

Support a Child Advocacy Group

Invite a representative from a local or state coalition or organization that advocates on behalf of children. (Contact CDF for a list of state groups.) Ask them to make a brief presentation about the work of their group and how people can support it. If appropriate, have a sign-up sheet for new members, sample copies of newsletters or action alerts, and a means of making donations.

Conduct a Public Witness

Place a spotlight on children's needs and urge action through some form of public witness. Possibilities include a march from your congregation's building to a symbolic location such as the town hall or a child-serving center, a rally with speakers, or a silent, candlelit gathering or bell-ringing, coordinated with other congregations in town. Carry placards or banners that raise awareness of the problems facing children and call for action. Be clear about your objectives as you plan. Do you want to raise awareness in the community? Do you want to put pressure on elected officials to take an action? Do you want to demonstrate support for or oppose a policy or program? Contact the media in advance (see Section 2 for suggestions) to help focus attention on your action.

Be a Voice for Children at a Letter-Writing Table

Set up a table with writing supplies (paper, envelopes, stamps, and pens) and sample letters or information to assist people in advocating on behalf of children. See suggestions and a sample letter in this section. If there is a Washington, D.C., office of your denomination or faith group that works on public policy issues, they may have materials to help you as well. The week before the Children's Sabbath, visit CDF's Web site at www.childrensdefense.org for the latest action alerts, or call our Religious Affairs Division at (202) 662-3589. Invite members to write letters to members of Congress urging them to help ensure that every child has a Healthy Start, a Head Start, a Fair Start, a Safe Start, and a Moral Start in life. If they wish, invite them to read their letters aloud in order to share their concern and inspire others. Include drawing paper and crayons so that young children can draw pictures depicting their hopes or concerns for children, or have younger children dictate their letters. Older children and youths can write their own letters. Consider having a delegation from the congregation (including children, youths, and adults) hand-deliver the letters to your member of Congress in the local district office. If you do this, use the occasion to focus media attention on children's concerns. (See the suggestions in Section 2 for contacting the media to solicit coverage.)

Plan a Visit to Your Legislators

Meeting with legislators face-to-face is one of the most effective ways that you can be a witness for children and advocate on their behalf. However, such advocacy is new and intimidating for many people. Hold a session to explain the basics of meeting with legislators and to plan a visit to address children's needs. (Use the guide in this section to help you plan your visit.) If possible, invite a speaker from an advocacy organization or a congregation member experienced in making lobbying visits to facilitate the planning session, and to lead the group in its meeting with the legislator.

Write a Letter to the Editor

Have copies of local newspapers from the past few weeks. Encourage people to identify articles on children, health, early childhood development, child care, education, poverty, violence, and other related issues. Then, invite them to write a letter to the editor which responds to the article and uses it as an opportunity to inform readers about the challenges facing children and needed responses. Print the tips on the following page on a poster or a flyer at the table so that people can refer to them while writing.

TIPS ON WRITING A LETTER TO THE EDITOR

(Adapted from *Reclaiming Our Democracy: Healing the Break Between People and Government,* by Sam Harris)

- **Respond to a recent news story or editorial.** A good letter might begin, "Your article on the new poverty statistics ("Poverty Rate is Increasing, Oct. 4") was excellent. Readers might want to know that..." You don't have to agree with the article, editorial, or column. Say respectfully whether you think they got the story right or not, and assert your views.

- **Make your letter short** (no more than a few paragraphs, about 300 words) and legible. It should contain a few striking facts that might surprise an editor or a reader. ("The staggering U.S. child poverty rate is leaving behind 13.5 million children and—if unaddressed—will leave our nation behind in the new millennium. Children growing up in poverty lag behind their peers in health, safety, and education.")

- **Use descriptive words** that communicate how passionately you feel about the issue. Don't be dry. ("When I look into the trusting brown eyes of a child whose family has come to the [Mytown Congregation] food pantry, I know that the increasing poverty rate is counted not in numbers but in lives....")

- **Include your address and home and work phone numbers.**

TIPS ON WRITING A LETTER TO YOUR MEMBER OF CONGRESS

- **Be brief.** Address only one issue. A letter need not be longer than four or five sentences.

- **Be specific.** If you are writing about specific legislation, include its bill number or title.

- **Write your own letter,** adapting a sample letter as appropriate. Form letters do not receive the same attention as individually written letters.

- **Be positive and constructive**. Try to say something complimentary in the first paragraph. It is just as important to thank members of Congress for voting the right way as it is to express your disappointment when you feel they have voted the wrong way.

- **Say in your own words** why the legislation matters to you and to children. Clearly state your reason for supporting or opposing the bill or issue you are writing about.

- **If you have particular knowledge or expertise, describe it.** Relating the bill to local or state conditions is especially effective.

- **If you wish, include a copy of a report,** a newsletter story, or a local survey to support your arguments. Don't presume that the legislator is aware of such information, even if you think it is common knowledge.

- **Be sure to sign your name legibly and include your address** so your Representative or Senator can respond.

For the latest information on legislation and needed action, visit the Children's Defense Fund's Web site at www.childrensdefense.org, or call CDF's Religious Affairs Division at (202) 662-3589.

SAMPLE LETTER STEP BY STEP

(Please note: The examples written in the parentheses are meant as examples only. Write your letter in your own words to reflect your concerns, experience, and perspective.)

The Honorable _____   Or: The Honorable _____
United States Senate   House of Representatives
Washington, DC 20510   Washington, DC 20515

Dear Senator: Or: Dear Representative:

1. Introduce Yourself. (My name is Janet Doe, and I am a member of Mytown Congregation in Mytown. I appreciate your commitment to public service.)

2. Share Your Concern for Children. (I am writing because I care about the millions of American children who are being left behind. More than 13.5 million children live in poverty, 11.9 million children lack health insurance, 13 million young children are in child care, and 5 million children are left alone after school where they are at risk of unsafe behavior such as drinking, drug use, crime, violence, and too early sexual activity. We see these problems in Mytown. Here, our food pantries can't keep up with the need of all the Mytown families struggling in poverty.)

3. Share Your Vision for Children. (I am committed to a community, state, and nation that gives every child a Healthy Start, a Head Start, a Fair Start, a Safe Start, and a Moral Start in life. Everyone—parents, congregations, schools, businesses, community, and government at all levels—has a role to play.)

4. Talk About the Solutions and Urge Action on Them. (Despite the magnitude of the problems affecting millions of children, there are proven, cost-effective ways to give all children the start in life they need and deserve, such as preventive and sick care for children, safe, affordable, quality child care programs and Head Start programs, adequate income and income supports for families, and after-school programs to keep older children safe and engaged in constructive activities. I hope that you will vote for [number and title of legislation] to [describe what it would do].)

5. Thank the Representative and Ask for a Reply. (Thank you for your attention to my concern that we leave no child behind and give every child the start in life he or she deserves. I look forward to your reply informing me of how you will address these concerns.)

Sincerely,

Your name
Your address
Your telephone number

How to address your envelope:

The Honorable _____   Or: The Honorable_____
United States Senate   House of Representatives
Washington, DC 20510   Washington, DC 20515

MEETING WITH YOUR LEGISLATORS

Before Your Visit

Begin planning for your visit. Don't worry if you have butterflies in your stomach at the thought of meeting with your legislator for the first time. It would be unusual if you didn't. Know that the best way to communicate with your legislator is to make a personal visit, and you probably will enjoy the experience—and the legislator will appreciate the time you spent communicating your views. So take a deep breath and begin planning! First, decide on the issues you want to discuss.

Make an appointment. When making an appointment, explain what issue you would like to discuss. If the legislator is unavailable, the aide who deals with your issue often will be knowledgeable and instrumental in helping to form the member's views. Don't feel slighted if you end up meeting with the aide. He or she can be very influential and, if your meeting goes well, may also encourage your legislator to meet with you in person the next time.

Do your homework. Study the legislator's voting record on a number of issues, using CDF's nonpartisan Congressional Voting Record and other sources, so you can comment on something positive, if possible, and know if the legislator tends to agree or disagree with you on this issue. If there is a bill that interests you, know its status and whether your legislator has taken a position on it.

Remember the experts! Parents, grandparents, service providers, educators, religious and business leaders, police officers, doctors and nurses, and others who witness children's needs on a daily basis are children's best advocates. They really are the experts when it comes to how bills and policies will affect children, and it's important that policy makers have a wide variety of people to call upon when they have questions about their work's impact on children. Children's advocacy groups often seek out these everyday experts to present the most compelling information during legislative visits. Share personal experiences you have had, if possible, to illustrate your point.

Be prepared. Before meeting with the legislator or aide, plan and organize your presentation, and practice what you are going to say. If you are going with other people to the meeting, get together beforehand to make sure that you all have the same purpose. Take along helpful information to back up your arguments: newspaper articles about the problems children face, statistics, or a fact sheet. (CDF can provide some of the information you need. Call the Religious Affairs Division at 202-662-3589 or visit CDF's Web site at www.childrensdefense.org).

During Your Visit

Make your message concise. You may think your meeting is for 30 minutes and then arrive to find the representative's schedule so tight that you get only five minutes. Know exactly what you want to say and be prepared to say it quickly, if needed.

Present solutions. People often feel overwhelmed by problems they consider too massive and diverse for corrective action, so don't just talk about the problem. Share one or two concrete ideas for ways to improve the lives of children in your community. Tell your representatives what it will take to ensure that no child is left behind.

Talk about what works. Using success stories of real children and families who are being helped by Head Start, child care, job training, or health insurance will strengthen your argument and counter claims that all government programs are ineffective.

Search for common ground. Don't be exclusive or judgmental. Keeping in mind the wide range of viewpoints in Congress and in every community and state legislature, frame your messages carefully to include words and themes that will reach new audiences and persuade them to become new allies. Children's advocates care as much as anyone about efficiency, accountability, fiscal responsibility, and personal responsibility. Use themes like these to frame your message.

Be honest. It's fine to say you don't know the answer to a question and to promise to provide information later, by phone, fax, or mail. This also gives you another opportunity to contact the office.

Following Your Visit

Build a relationship. The better your communication, the more seriously you will be taken, and the more willing the legislator and his or her staff will be to rely upon you and your judgments.

- Follow up your visit with a letter thanking the legislator for the time spent listening to your concerns. Enclose any documentation you had agreed to provide to bolster your position, and briefly restate your views.
- Send articles, write letters with further information, or offer your assistance in thinking through solutions that could work in your community.
- Call periodically with updates.
- Invite the legislator or the staff person who handles children's issues to speak before your congregation or a community group in which you are involved.
- Invite the legislator to visit a successful child-serving program with which you work, such as a child care program, after-school program, or Head Start class.

Show broad support for your concerns. If your legislator or aide disagrees or is noncommittal, don't threaten or argue after you have made your case because it is counterproductive. A better strategy is to plan another visit with others to show more community support for your position, to put together a group of letters from constituents, or to think of another tactic, such as a letter to the editor. Persistence often pays.

Watch how your legislator votes, and respond. If the legislator votes with your position on the issue, recognize that vote with a written "thank-you." Such recognition may influence his or her next vote on children's issues. It also lets your legislator know that you are watching closely. If the legislator votes against your position, write or call to express your disappointment, and urge reconsideration of the issue the next time it comes up for a vote.

Follow-Up Actions and Resources for All Faiths

At its best, the Children's Sabbath weekend serves to launch and inspire new, long-term efforts to help children. Children's needs extend long past the weekend itself, and so should our faithful response.

Listed below are pointers to consider as you select a follow-up project, followed by many ideas for efforts that congregations may undertake. The ideas are grouped by area of concern: suggestions for giving every child a Healthy Start, a Head Start, a Fair Start, a Safe Start, and a Moral Start. A last category, "Leave No Child Behind," provides comprehensive suggestions that cut across the five "starts." In addition to follow-up ideas in each area, we have suggested publications, videos, and organizations that may be helpful resources. The resources from the Children's Defense Fund are available through the order form at the back of this manual.

- **Begin planning for the follow-up while you are planning the rest of your Children's Sabbath activities**. Don't wait until the Children's Sabbath weekend is over, when the planning team may need a break. Also, you want to secure participants' commitments for follow-up while their enthusiasm and attention are strong.

- **If possible, offer a range of follow-up opportunities to meet the varied interests and abilities of your congregation members.** Ideally, there should be the chance to help raise awareness, to provide hands-on service, and to advocate on children's behalf. The symbols by each suggestion below will help you consider a range of options. (An ear/eye=raise awareness; a hand=hands-on service; a mouth=advocacy.)

- **Remember that some long-term commitments may be made by individual members, while others will represent the investment of the congregation as a whole.** Your Children's Sabbath may offer the opportunity for both. For new congregational programs or commitments, be sure to secure the necessary approval of clergy, staff, and/or appropriate committees.

- **Look for ways to reinforce good existing efforts for children in your congregation and community.** Your follow-up program does not have to be started from scratch, if there are already good things being done by community organizations or other congregations. Find out what is happening to help you decide whether to reinforce existing work or start a new program in your congregation.

- **Connect with your faith group's resources and efforts to improve the lives of children.** Many denominations and other faith groups have terrific publications, videos, newsletters, and other resources to support congregations and individuals who are working with and for children. Further, there are a number of exciting child advocacy campaigns, networks, and programs in place at the national and regional level of many religious bodies. Some of these are listed at the end of this resource section. Find out what is happening in your religious group, and draw on those resources.

• **Provide support to help people fulfill their new commitments.** Maintain a list of those who are volunteering in follow-up efforts, and then give them a call or drop them a note to let them know their commitment matters and the congregation is there to support them. Recognize them in a bulletin or newsletter. At the next Children's Sabbath, honor those who have given a year of service as a result of the previous Children's Sabbath.

Give Every Child a Healthy Start

 Start a "Drive So They'll Thrive" Program. Organize volunteers to transport pregnant women and parents and children to and from local health clinics that provide prenatal and pediatric care. Work with clinics to advertise the availability of the free transportation and to schedule it at appropriate times.

 Help Children While Away the Wait. Set up and staff a play area in a health clinic or WIC (Special Supplemental Nutrition Program for Women, Infants, and Children) program office for children waiting with family members.

 Make Sure No One Is Turned Away. Work with local, public, and religious-affiliated hospitals to develop arrangements that will enable pregnant women who lack health insurance to get hospital care for their deliveries.

 Encourage Investment in Children's Health. Help generate business and corporate support for community groups working to improve the health of infants and children.

 Help Children Get Health Insurance. Be a voice in your community and state to help uninsured children get health care. Most states now offer free or low-cost health insurance to children in working families with incomes up to $33,400 for a family of four. Your congregation can let families know they are eligible and get them enrolled. For information about how you can help, contact CDF at 1-800-CDF-1200 ext. 2, or visit the Sign Them Up section of CDF's Web site at www.childrensdefense/signup.org. This area of the Web site has updated information about successful outreach efforts across the country, as well as detailed information about each state's Children's Health Insurance and Medicaid programs and links to state Web pages and applications.

Resources

Insuring Children's Health: A Community Guide to Enrolling Children in Free and Low-Cost Health Insurance Programs, CDF, 1999. First five copies free, $2.00 each for additional copies. This community guide is designed to help communities across the country inform families about and enroll children in the new State Children's Health Insurance Program (CHIP) and Medicaid. The guide provides easy, step-by-step information about how to involve schools, the child care community, the faith-based community, and others in local efforts to enroll children. It provides state-by-state income eligibility tables, flyers in both Spanish and English, talking points, frequently-asked questions, and more.

Maternal and Child Health Ministry: A Bibliography of Resources for the Religious Community. Free. Volume II of the Justice of Children and Their Families Bibliographic Series, this 15-page resource provides an introductory essay on the ministry of health and healing, a listing of many denominational resolutions on health care concerns, and a list of resources on health ministries produced by denominations and other groups. Available from the National Council of the Churches of Christ in the U.S.A. Ask for PDS 72-650-95-004. Call 1-800-524-2612.

The Health Cabinet, by Jill Westberg MacNamara. $6.00 for a single copy, discounts for orders of five or more. Explores the varieties of health ministries, the history of the church and healing, and the theology of health ministries. Practical "how to" section outlines process of creating a health cabinet, surveying your congregation, and organizing a health ministry step by step. Available from the National Parish Nurse Resource Center, 205 West Tuohy, Park Ridge, IL 60068.

Give Every Child a Head Start

Extend a Welcome. Invite the families of children attending Head Start or child care programs and children being cared for at home by their parents to attend free or low-cost activities sponsored by your congregation.

Get to Know Your Child Care Program. If your congregation already houses a child care program, discuss with the director how it can become more visible to the congregation. Perhaps a small bulletin board could display class photographs, with a description of the program and periodic events or needs. Invite the director to tell the congregation about the curriculum and how it helps children at a gathering after services or in updates posted on the bulletin board.

Promote Play and Perhaps Pray. Begin a playgroup for children and their stay-at-home parents, or invite an existing group to use your facilities (such as a playground, toys, or large room to meet in). Another model is a "Pray and Play" group during which at-home parents gather for prayer and reflection while the children are cared for by others at the congregation.

Forge a Partnership. Enter into a partnership with a congregation providing child care and Head Start for low-income families. Provide toys and equipment, financial support, or volunteer assistance. You can also call your local Head Start center directly to find out what kind of help from the community is needed.

House a Child Care Program. Develop or house an after-school child care program, a full-day child care program, or a Head Start program in your congregation's building. Excellent resources to assist you are available from the Ecumenical Child Care Network (address listed under resources below).

Champion Child Care Causes in Congress. Write to your members of Congress about child care needs in your community and urge them to increase funding for Head Start and child care. Do the same with your state legislators. States can invest in child care, prekindergarten, Head Start, and after-school programs. Let your state legislators know how important this funding is. For up-to-date legislative information, visit CDF's Web site at www.childrensdefense.org and click on "Head Start" on our home page.

Support After-School and Summer Programs. Help children keep learning, make good choices, and interact with positive role models after school and during the summer. Find out what after-school and summer programs currently exist in your community. If good ones are in place, find out how your congregation can support them with one-time or regular volunteers, by giving donations or supplies, or by encouraging children to participate. If good programs are in short supply, explore how your congregation could help get one started.

Start a Summer Freedom School or After-School Program. Freedom Schools, developed by the Black Community Crusade for Children (BCCC), provide academic and cultural enrichment, recreation, and nutrition to children during the summer and throughout the year after school. To date BCCC has trained more than 2,500 college-aged servant-leaders who have taught more than 12,000 children, ages 5 to 16, in their local community Freedom School programs. For more information, call BCCC at (202) 628-8787.

Resources

Key Facts: Essential Information on Child Care, Early Education, and School Age Care. CDF, 191 pp., 1999. $5.95. This briefing book contains a series of fact sheets about child care, early education, and school-age care, as well as data and material about policies and programs. It is designed to provide useful information in a format that can be easily adapted to various individual and organizational needs.

State Child Care and Early Education Developments: Highlights and Updates for 1999. CDF, 124 pp., 2000. $7.95. This annual update of state actions on child care and early education issues examines changes in funding, eligibility, payment rates, quality initiatives, licensing, prekindergarten and State Head Start programs, and more, updating the information published in 1998.

Seeds of Success: State Prekindergarten Initiatives, 1998-1999. CDF, 226 pp., 1999. $9.95. What is your state doing to provide prekindergarten for its children? How does your state's prekindergarten initiative compare to those in other states? This report is an update of an earlier CDF study. It provides state officials, advocates, and others interested in early care and education with an overview of state efforts to support prekindergarten initiatives. It examines the progress states have made over the past decade in ensuring that high quality prekindergarten is available and accessible to children and in integrating their prekindergarten initiatives with other early childhood supports. It also considers further steps states can take to strengthen their initiatives.

Summer Freedom School and After-School Curriculum Guides and Book List, and Latino Freedom School Supplement and Book List, CDF. Curriculum Guide $30.00, Freedom School Curriculum Guide with Latino Supplement, $50.00, After-School Curriculum Guide, $30.00, Freedom School Book List, $5.00. These curriculum guides and lesson plans incorporate the latest research and best practices in academic and cultural enrichment, recreation, and nutrition programs for children. They include carefully selected books and activities designed to excite and motivate, allowing children to discover their individual identities and talents.

Helping Churches Mind the Children: A Guide for Church-Housed Child Care Programs. National Council of the Churches of Christ, 51 pp., 1987. $7.00 for Ecumenical Child Care Network members, $9.00 for non-members. This booklet provides a format and practical suggestions for assessing the need for a congregational child care program and how to

initiate, publicize, and resource the program. To order, call the Ecumenical Child Care Network.

Policy Statement on Child Day Care. National Council of the Churches of Christ in the U.S.A.. $0.75 for Ecumenical Child Care Network members, $1.00 for non-members. Statement issued by the governing board of the National Council of the Churches of Christ in the U.S.A. that provides a strong theological and pragmatic basis for provision of high quality church-based child care. To order, call 1-800-649-5443.

Statement on Quality Child Care. Women's League for Conservative Judaism. To order, call (212) 628-1600.

Let the Children Come to Me: A Statement on Early Childhood Care and Education. U.S. Catholic Conference. Call 1-800-235-8722.

Organizations

Ecumenical Child Care Network, 8765 W. Higgins Rd., Suite 405, Chicago, IL 60631, 1-800-649-5443. The Ecumenical Child Care Network (ECCN) addresses church-based child care and offers an organizational structure that can bring about change and development in the area of church-based care. ECCN connects church-sponsored and church-housed child care providers to each other and to a variety of supportive resources, including a newsletter, other publications, and an annual conference.

Jewish Childcare Association, 575 Lexington Ave., New York, NY 10022. (212) 371-1313.

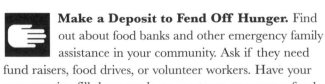

Give Every Child a Fair Start

 Learn More and Spread the Word. Read and share newspaper articles about child poverty and family income issues. Include basic facts or short articles about child poverty and family income in your congregation's bulletin or newsletter.

Make a Deposit to Fend Off Hunger. Find out about food banks and other emergency family assistance in your community. Ask if they need fund raisers, food drives, or volunteer workers. Have your congregation fill these needs, or create an emergency fund or food bank of its own to help families get through times of crisis.

 Help Families Get Credit. Inform eligible families in your congregation and community about the Earned Income Tax Credit (EITC), a federal tax credit worth up to $3,000 or more for low-income working families with children. To learn how you can publicize the EITC and to receive outreach posters and other materials, contact the Center on Budget and Policy Priorities, 820 First Street, N.E., Suite 510, Washington, DC 20002, (202) 408-1080.

 Help Make Employment Work for Parents. Talk with local nonprofit agencies that provide job training about how to help unemployed and underemployed families in your congregation and community find jobs. Arrange transportation and child care to allow parents to go to interviews, attend education and job training, and keep their jobs. (See child care suggestions above.)

 Extend a Helping Hand to a Youth. Provide youths with internships and job mentoring through the congregation or members' places of employment. Work with the local schools, Boys and Girls Club, Big Brothers/Big Sisters, or other organizations to identify young people in need to support in order to help them develop job skills and confidence in their future employment.

  Spotlight the Impact of Poverty in Your Community. CDF's Community Monitoring Project is designed to help those working on behalf of children in states and communities use a simple survey process to document what works for families as well as the real-life consequences of inadequate and diminishing community supports. It also focuses on helping community members become more effective at sharing this information with the broader public and key constituencies. Through the project, CDF offers five types of support: written materials, skills-building workshops and training, individualized assistance, linkages to other advocacy and community monitoring efforts, and information collected by others. For more information about how you can get involved, call CDF at (202) 662-3552 or e-mail cdfmonitor@ childrensdefense.org.

 Call for Wise Investments to Help Families Work. Billions of dollars that are intended to help poor families with children move from welfare to work remain unspent. These funds can be used for purposes ranging from wage supplementation to child care to transportation. Connect with an advocacy organization in your community or state to help advocate that these funds be spent wisely. If you need help finding such an organization in your state, contact CDF's Family Income Division at (202) 628-8787.

Resources

Poverty Matters: The Cost of Child Poverty in America, CDF, 43 pp., 1997. $4.95. This report shatters the myth that America can ignore children in poverty, "the least of these," and find long-term prosperity. Contains key findings, recommendations, and hard-hitting anecdotes that put a face on poverty and associated problems from lead paint poisoning to substandard housing to learning disabilities.

A Parent's Guide to Child Support, CDF, 40 pp., 1999. $3.50. Because children need support from both parents, and our country's record has been unimpressive when it comes to enforcement of child support, CDF has developed a step-by-step guidebook to help parents maneuver through the bureaucratic maze. Discusses how to establish paternity and pursue interstate cases, and reviews changes in the law related to the 1996 welfare law.

Welfare to What? Early Findings on Family Hardship and Well-Being, CDF and the National Coalition for the Homeless, 68 pp., 1998. $2.50. This report takes a deeper look at evidence of family well-being, drawing on new national survey data, review of status by state, and private research institutions, and a compilation of findings from informal community-based monitoring, among other sources. It presents a mixed and troubling picture, identifying some successful efforts worthy of replication, but also sounding the alarm about rising hardship and an increase in extreme childhood poverty.

Head Start: Helping Families Move from Welfare to Work, CDF, 24 pp., 1998. $3.95. This report focuses on the efforts of Head Start to help parents gain the confidence and skills needed to successfully move from welfare to work. Includes profiles of individuals and measures their success; also outlines stumbling blocks and how to avoid them. A practical resource for advocates assisting parents with job training and support.

Poverty and Faithjustice: An Adult Program for Dialogue on Christian Discipleship in the United States. U.S. Catholic Conference, 24 pp., $1.95. Available in English and Spanish. This resource provides sessions designed to give participants an opportunity to get in touch with their attitudes and ways of thinking about poverty and to become aware of and to understand faithjustice as the virtue promoting a just society based on Christian faith in God's vision of human life. To order, call 1-800-235-8722.

Tough Choices: Jewish Perspectives on Social Justice, by David Vorspan and David Saperstein. Union of American Hebrew Congregations. Confronts social justice dilemmas and the hard, cutting-edge issues of our time, guided by Jewish sources and texts. Has extensive material on economic justice issues. To order, call (212) 249-0100.

Give Every Child a Safe Start

Observe Child Abuse Prevention Month. April is Child Abuse Prevention Month. Sponsor a special program to educate your congregation about child abuse and other domestic violence and steps that can be taken to prevent it and to assist families where abuse has occurred.

Provide a Safe Space. Establish a place at your congregation where birth parents can visit with their children who are in foster care in comfortable surroundings. Senior citizens could be available to assist local social workers with transportation for both the foster children and their birth parents. Together with teens from the youth group, they also might provide on-site child care.

Start a Neighborhood Watch. Organize your congregation for a more active presence on the streets of the neighborhood. A neighborhood watch group offers an opportunity for residents to get to know each other and to look out for one another, resulting in a safer community. For more information about starting or joining a neighborhood watch group, contact your local police department and the National Crime Prevention Council at (202) 466-6272.

Establish Safe Corridors. Many children are concerned about their personal safety as they go to and from school. Organizations, including congregations, have partnered with schools in their communities to recruit and train volunteers to escort children to and from school. In addition, some congregations have opened their doors to provide safe havens for children in the event of some threat to their safety.

Speak Out to Keep Children Safe. Advocate for sensible gun regulation and for increased investments in initiatives that promote the positive development of youths. Visit CDF's Web site at www.childrensdefense.org and click on "Safe Start" for action alerts and other information about legislation to keep children safe. Be sure to click on CDF's "Youth Violence Resource Center" for more information and for instructions on joining CDF's Violence Prevention listserv. Also, display CDF's Safe Start Campaign posters in your congregation's building, and explore having these public education materials displayed throughout your community.

Establish Grounds for Peace. Put up a sign that indicates that no firearms are to be carried on the grounds of your congregation. Keep the space sacred and a haven from violence.

Establish and maintain a memorial for children who are victims of guns and other violence in your community. Communities across the country are developing creative and moving memorials for the children who have been killed. Among them are displaying shoes (one pair for each child killed) on the steps of congregational buildings, displaying flowers or ribbons, tolling bells every two hours to remind the community that that is how often a child is killed by gunfire in this country, or building a peace statue out of toys collected at a violent toy trade-in. Choose a fitting memorial and publicize it. Let the community know that the children will not be forgotten and that your place of worship will establish and maintain a space for remembering the children and making sure the community does not forget.

Turn Off the Violence. Participate in this campaign to encourage families to turn away from violence-oriented entertainment and toward fun alternatives. Turn Off the Violence (TOV) is designated for October 14, but the approach to more positive, peaceful entertainment is encouraged throughout the year. For more information, contact TOV at P.O. Box 27558, Minneapolis, MN 55427, (612) 593-8041.

Resources

Children and Guns: A Children's Defense Fund Report on Children Dying from Gunfire in America. Children's Defense Fund, 65 pp., 1999. Free. Escalating violence against and by children and youths is no coincidence. It is the manifestation of a range of serious and too-long neglected problems. Factors such as poverty, economic inequality, racial intolerance, drug and alcohol abuse, domestic violence, violent images in our popular culture, and the availability of deadly firearms all contribute to the prevalence of violence in our communities. *Children and Guns* takes a closer look at these factors and provides the latest statistics on national trends and state action. Recommended action steps for parents and grandparents, educators, religious leaders, and community leaders are provided.

Violence brochure. CDF, revised 1999. Free. This informative and motivational brochure outlines the parameters of the crises killing children, debunks ten myths about guns, provides survey data on public support for gun control measures, suggests ten steps to stop the violence against children, lists a range of resources to support efforts to keep children safe, and offers a Pledge for Children and a response form to get involved.

Hear Their Cries: Religious Responses to Child Abuse (video, 48 minutes), Center for the Prevention of Sexual and Domestic Violence. $129.00. This documentary addresses the role of religious communities in preventing all forms of child abuse: physical, sexual, and emotional. Comes with a study guide and awareness brochures. For shipping and handling costs, more information, or to preview, rent, or purchase resources, call (206) 634-1903 ext. 11 or visit the Web site at www.cpsdv.org.

Creating Circles of Peace: Alternatives to Violence Kits, Institute for Peace and Justice. English version $59.95, Spanish version $29.95. Available in English and Spanish, these kits for Christian churches offer the tools to do something positive about violence, helping both adults and children learn skills for resolving conflicts nonviolently and challenging violence in the media, community, and sometimes even in school and at home. The kits provide practical and engaging activities for implementing a Family Pledge of Non-Violence, bulletin inserts, workshop and retreat outlines, a newsletter, and more. To order, call 1-800-833-0245.

Introductory Packets on Families Against Violence, Institute for Peace and Justice. $6.00 each. These packets for Jewish Congregations, Muslim Ummahs, Buddhist Communities, Baha'i Communities, and Unitarian Communities contain the Pledge of Nonviolence, a Families Creating a Circle of Peace booklet, an appropriate prayer card, "Six Steps to Develop a Commitment to Stand Against Violence," and other items that make the program especially appropriate for each faith tradition. To order, call 1-800-833-0245.

Parent Action Kit, The Lion & Lamb Project. $12.00 contribution per kit requested. The main resource from the Lion & Lamb Project, the Parent Action Kit is an easy-to-read guide that recently won the Parents' Choice Award. The Kit includes three small folders, each containing a section on *What You Should Know* and *What You Can Do*. The Kit gives guidance for selecting age-appropriate, nonviolent toys and

games; suggests helpful books and organizations; and provides tips for resolving family conflicts peacefully. To order, call (301) 654-3091, visit the Web site www.lionlamb.org, or mail your order, with a check made payable to The Lion & Lamb Project/Tides Center (see Organizations below).

Blessed Are the Peacemakers (video, 60 minutes). U.S. Bishops' Catholic Communication Campaign. This video presentation shows three communities where individuals are taking action to stop violence in their communities and in their lives. Visit New Orleans, where a multi-denominational organization called ACT (All Congregations Together) is determined to purge the neighborhood of drugs, guns, and delinquent landlords. Then travel to Los Angeles, where programs called Hope In Youth and Jobs for the Future are working to keep young people from joining gangs by providing one-on-one counseling, positive role models, and educational support. To order, call 1-800-235-8722.

Organizations

Center for the Prevention of Sexual and Domestic Violence, 936 N. 34th Street, Suite 200, Seattle, WA 98103, (206) 634-1903. E-mail: cpsdv@cpsdv.org; Web site: www.cpsdv.org. An interreligious educational resource serving both religious and secular communities, the Center provides training workshops, conferences, books, videos, curricula, and a newsletter.

Institute for Peace and Justice, 4144 Lindell Boulevard, #408, St. Louis, MO 63108, (314) 533-4445. E-mail: ppjn@aol.com. The Institute for Peace and Justice coordinates the Parenting for Peace and Justice Network and the Families Against Violence Network, both of which offer tools, skills, and a support network. While many of the resources are for Christian churches, the Institute has also developed resources for Jewish, Muslim, Buddhist, Baha'i, and Unitarian Universalist congregations and communities.

The Lion & Lamb Project, 4300 Montgomery Ave., Suite 104, Bethesda, MD 20814, (301) 654-3091. E-mail: lionlamb@lionlamb.org. Web site: www.lionlamb.org. The Lion & Lamb Project is an initiative by parents for parents, helping families find alternatives to violent toys, games, and entertainment. The Project provides parents with information about the ways young children learn violent behaviors from television, movies, arcade and video games, action figures, and other violent toys and "entertainment." The Lion & Lamb's main resource is the Parent Action Kit, an easy-to-read guide that recently won the Parents' Choice Award. Lion & Lamb also offers parenting workshops nationwide, and co-sponsors events such as Violent Toy Trade-Ins.

Give Every Child a Moral Start

 Become a Mentor. Encourage congregation members to become mentors to children in need of positive, supportive, caring role models. Contact the local chapter of Big Brothers/Big Sisters, Inc..

 Arrange Families Care Days. One of the best ways for children to learn compassion, generosity, and other positive values is to see adults put them into practice. One weekend a month (or quarterly), arrange an opportunity for all ages to work together to meet a need in the community. This may be preparing a meal at a soup kitchen, helping build a Habitat for Humanity house, cleaning up a playground, or painting over graffiti.

 Draw Up a Community Covenant for Children. Working with area schools, convene parents to draft a simple community covenant which parents would voluntarily sign. Such a covenant could include commitments not to serve alcoholic beverages at teen parties in your home and not to permit parties in your home without a responsible adult present. While parents may choose not to sign the covenant, those who do may know that their child is safer when attending gatherings at the homes of others who have signed. The process of drafting the covenant may be a helpful process in identifying and clarifying shared community values, and may convey common expectations to the children.

 Sponsor Parent Workshops and Parenting Circles. Parents urgently need opportunities to share questions and experiences on the joys and challenges of raising children—including how to teach children positive values in a commercial and violent culture. Arrange a short-term course or an ongoing group, with separate sessions for parents of young children, elementary school children, and teenagers. Poll parents in your congregation to find out what day of the week and time work best. Invite parents in the community to participate. Consider providing child care during the meetings to make it easier for parents to participate.

Challenge the Media to Become a Partner in Teaching Positive Values to Young People. Work with other congregations to develop creative strategies to draw attention to—and challenge—the negative values and violence promoted by the media. Help children and adults strengthen their media literacy and critical media skills. Contact the Center for Media Literacy, 4727 Wilshire Boulevard, Suite 403, Los Angeles, CA 90010, (323) 931-4177, www.medialit.org.

Sponsor a Beat the Odds® Celebration of Children's Strengths. Millions of our children are staying in school, are not on drugs or in gangs, and are struggling to succeed despite the decay and disarray around them. Let's celebrate them! CDF founded Beat the Odds celebrations in 1990. Over the past 10 years, communities across the country have hosted events honoring young people who are beating the odds. These inspiring evenings focus community and media attention on the positive accomplishments of young people. If you are interested in sponsoring a Beat the Odds celebration in your city, call CDF and the Black Community Crusade for Children at (202) 628-8787 for a how-to manual to help you.

 **Have "Invite a Friend" or "Come As You Are" Days.** Quarterly, have an "Invite a Friend Day" at your congregation. Encourage adults and children alike to invite friends to attend services and congregational activities with them. On these days, make sure that rituals and routines that the congregation takes for granted are explained if possible (marking "sit" or "stand" in the bulletin, announcing the page number in a worship book and allowing extra time for people to find it, writing out common prayers that others have memorized, and so forth). Some congregations sponsor "Come As You Are" days when they attend worship in more casual attire than their usual finery. They have found this encourages neighborhood youths to feel less intimidated about attending.

Resources

Lanterns: A Memoir of Mentors, Marian Wright Edelman, 180 pp., 1999. $20.00. Marian Wright Edelman, the founder and president of the Children's Defense Fund, shares powerful stories about the mentors in her life, from her childhood through the Civil Rights Movement to the founding and building of CDF. She pays tribute to the extraordinary personal mentors who helped light her way: Martin Luther King, Jr., Robert F. Kennedy, Fannie Lou Hamer, William Sloane Coffin, Ella Baker, Mae Bertha Carter, and many others. She brings home the importance of mentoring, caring about, and standing for children every day.

The Measure of Our Success: A Letter to My Children and Yours, Marian Wright Edelman, 97 pp., 1992. $12.00 hardcover, $9.00 audiotape. Marian Wright Edelman's touching and moral message to her sons—a message both introspective and compelling that all of us can use in our daily struggle to find the right balance. She passes on a family legacy based on service to others, and the 25 lessons for life she wants most to impart to her sons.

Grace to Lead Our Children Home: The Crisis Facing Black Children. CDF, 38 pp., 2000. $3.00. This manual is a product of CDF's Black Community Crusade for Children's Black Church Initiative. It describes the particular challenges facing Black children and gives suggestions for what Black churches can do to help—including profiles of programs at ten churches across the country that are making a difference.

A Lesson of Value: A Joint Statement on Moral Education in the Public Schools (brochure). $0.50. This joint statement from the U.S. Catholic bishops and the Synagogue Council of America affirms the need for schools, teachers, and parents to provide today's youths with a positive system of moral values as they face contemporary problems. To order, call 1-800-235-8722.

Family Guide for Using Media, National Conference of Catholic Bishops. No. 5-324, 8-panel brochure, $0.50. The U.S. bishops consider the increased accessibility of the internet, computer networks, and related media and their subsequent impact on people. In this updated edition, parents and others are encouraged to affirm Christian values when evaluating and making use of the tools of this expanding arena. Ten actions or attitudes are provided as a guide toward this goal. To order, call 1-800-235-8722.

Building Assets in Congregations: A Practical Guide for Helping Youth Grow Up Healthy, Search Institute, #113, 1998, 176 pp., $18.95. This guide offers everything you'll need to create a congregation that builds assets—young people's strengths. Perfect for youth workers, clergy, volunteers, and others, this practical book includes worksheets for assessing and planning your current priorities and programs, strategies and ideas for introducing assets into youth programs, tips for creating intergenerational programs and parent workshops, and ten reproducible bulletin inserts. To order, call 1-800-888-7828 or visit www.search-institute.org.

For the Children: Words of Love and Inspiration from His Holiness Pope John Paul II, Scholastic Press, 2000. 31 pp., $16.95 (softcover). This book features citations from twenty years of speeches and writings by John Paul II, many of them addressed specifically to children. Touching photographs complement his heartfelt statements on love, peace, education, family, prayer, and our responsibility to ensure a brighter future for children everywhere. To order, call 1-800-SCHOLASTIC.

Leave No Child Behind!

The following resources from a range of religious and secular groups address the many and varied needs of children and families and ways that congregations can develop comprehensive responses.

Resources from the Children's Defense Fund

Welcome the Child: A Child Advocacy Guide for Churches. CDF and Friendship Press, 1994, $9.95. This guide for clergy, staff, and everyone involved in ministering to children provides practical information for involving the congregation in child advocacy.

Guide My Feet: Prayers and Meditations on Loving and Working for Children. Beacon Press, 1995, 210 pp., $17.95. Marian Wright Edelman, president and founder of CDF, offers inspiration, prayers of thanksgiving, pleas for guidance, and pledges of commitment.

Bible with Child Advocate's Concordance. Thomas Nelson Publishers, $25.00. For faithful Christians who care about and work for children. This special edition of the New Revised Standard Version of the Bible includes a Child Advocate's Topical Concordance detailing references to children prepared by the Religious Affairs Division of the Children's Defense Fund and a message from Marian Wright Edelman. Bound in forest green leather, measures $4^{1/2}$" x $6^{1/2}$".

National Observance of Children's Sabbaths: Raising Voices, Linking Hands for Children (video, 9 minutes). CDF, $5.95. This video features highlights from Children's Sabbaths across the country, as well as interviews with a variety of religious leaders. Inspires communities of faith to participate in the Children's Sabbath and strengthen service and advocacy efforts for children.

A Prayer for Children (video, 3 minutes). CDF, $6.50. This moving poem by Ina Hughs is read by Marian Wright Edelman, with footage of children on an inspirational video that may be used in worship, educational programs, or to begin or end a meeting.

Welcoming the Children (video, 24 minutes.) CDF and Friendship Press, 1994, $29.95. This video shows how local congregations respond to urgent needs of children by using their own resources and forming partnerships with other groups. Accompanying study guide provides an outline for using with a single congregation or multiple congregations to plan strategies for helping children.

The State of America's Children Yearbook 2000. CDF, 2000, $15.95. CDF's annual analysis of the status of children in America, with the latest developments and data related to child poverty, family income, child health and the State Children's Health Insurance Program, child care, education, and juvenile justice. Forward by Marian Wright Edelman offers both vision and challenge.

Congressional Workbook 2000. CDF, 2000, 184 pp., $7.00. This basic process and issue primer gives you information about where to go, who to talk to, and how to work a legislative agenda. Included are key facts about the budget and appropriations process, how a bill becomes law, congressional subcommittees working on children's issues, a directory of House and Senate members, how to contact your member and others, a legislative glossary, and more.

Resources and Initiatives of Religious Organizations and Denominations:

Social Action Manual: A Practical Guide for Organizing and Programming Social Action in the Synagogue, Religious Action Center of Reform Judaism. A complete guide for congregations with descriptions of resources and social action organizations. To order, call (202) 387-2800.

Ani V'Atah: *How To Do Social Justice Programming* (video). A video exploring how to develop successful social justice activities in your congregation, including coalition building and advocacy. Available from the Religious Action Center of Reform Judaism. To order, call (202) 387-2800.

A Catholic Campaign for Children: Parish Resource Manual. This comprehensive resource includes practical planning and support materials, clip art, bulletin quotes, liturgical and preaching guides and models to hope parishes integrate a focus on children and families into all aspects of parish life. Includes the Bishops' Statement, "Putting Children and Families First: A Challenge for Our Church, Nation, and World," a resource developed by committees on domestic social policy, international policy, and marriage and family life. A video is also available. Also available in Spanish. Available from the U.S. Catholic Conference, 1-800-235-8722.

Renewing the Vision: A Framework for Catholic Youth Ministry. Available in English and Spanish, 61 pp., $4.95. The U.S. Roman Catholic bishops address the call to personal discipleship, evangelization, and leadership. Offered as a "blueprint" for the continued development of effective ministry with young and older adolescents, this framework is an affirmation of the faith, gifts, energy, and fresh ideas of young people, a Christ-centered vision, and a call to empower young people.

A Church for All God's Children, The United Methodist Church. In 1996, the Council of Bishops called upon The United Methodist Church to reshape its life in response to the crisis among children and the impoverished, and in faithfulness to Jesus Christ. Congregations are invited to undertake specific actions to make their churches more responsive to the needs of children and their families in the church and community. The packet *A Church for All God's Children* contains resources (checklist, guidelines, resource list, and reporting form) for churches that want to participate and to qualify as a "Church for All God's Children." The packet, which was sent to every United Methodist congregation, is available on The United Methodist Web site at www.umc.org/initiative.

Putting Children and Their Families First: A Planning Handbook for Congregations, General Board of Global Ministries, The United Methodist Church. $4.75 + postage and handling. This book offers strategies for assessing children's needs in the congregation and the community, identifying the strengths and assets of children, families, and communities, and developing a plan for comprehensive ministries. It also provides a biblical framework for ministry and suggestions for implementing new ministries. To order, call 1-800-305-9857.

Listen to the Children! (video, 35 minutes), The United Methodist Church. $12.50 + postage and handling. This video takes a look at the lives of children—their needs, fears, and hopes. To create this video, children at four church settings in diverse communities were given video cameras. Hear children's own messages to us through singing, dance, drama, and interviews. To order, call 1-800-305-9857.

Safe Haven for Children, Hope for Congregations and Communities, Evangelical Lutheran Church in America. A folder of tools and information to help Lutheran churches become "Safe Havens" for children in the community. Folder includes an emblem identifying the congregation as a Safe Haven for Children, a reproducible congregational resolution to become a Safe Haven, a certificate, and practical materials spelling out how congregations can be safe havens for children in poverty, needing child care, at risk of abuse, and more. Published by Augsburg Fortress Publishers, 1999. Web site: www.elca.org/init/safehaven.

Year of the Child, Presbyterian Church (U.S.A.). A brochure, newsletter, and range of other resources are available to help congregations participate in the General Assembly-designated "Year of the Child" (July 2000 to June 2001) and lift up the special gifts and needs of children and youths, birth to age eighteen, within the church, beyond the church, and throughout the world. For more information, call the Presbyterian Child Advocacy Office at (502) 569-5858 or write to The Year of the Child, The Child Advocacy Office, Presbyterian Church (U.S.A.), 100 Witherspoon Street, Louisville, KY 40202.

Organization

Stand for Children, 1834 Connecticut Ave., NW, Washington, DC 20009. Phone: 1-800-663-4032 or 202-234-0095, email: tellstand@stand.org. Web site: www.stand.org.

Copyright Credits

"Call to Worship" from the Presbyterian Women's Gathering 1991 and "Prayer of Confession" and "Assurance of Pardon" by Diana C. Austin—Reproduced from *Peacemaking Through Worship Volume II*, Jane Parker Huber, ed.. Published by the Presbyterian Peacemaking Program; Louisville, 1992. Used by permission.

"Call to Worship" by the Rev. Jon Schultz. Used by permission of the author.

"I Am Sent by God"—Reproduced from The Whole People of God Curriculum. Used by permission of Wood Lake Books Inc., Kelowna, British Columbia, Canada.

"Invitation to Prayer"—Reproduced from *More Than Words: Prayer and Ritual for Inclusive Communities* by Janet Schaffran and Pat Kozak. ©1988. Used by permission of the Crossroad Publishing Company, New York.

Prayers by Marian Wright Edelman from *Guide My Feet: Prayers and Meditations on Loving and Working For Children* by Marian Wright Edelman. ©1995 by Marian Wright Edelman. Reprinted by permission of Beacon Press, Boston.

"Renewal of Commitment"—Reproduced from *Banquet of Praise* by Bread for the World. ©1990 Bread for the World. Used by permission of Bread for the World.

Excerpts from the English translation of *The Roman Missal* © 1973, International Committee on English in the Liturgy, Inc.. All rights reserved.

"Take My Life, and Let It Be"—Reproduced from The United Methodist Hymnal. ©1989 The United Methodist Publishing House.

Evaluation Form

Let us know how you celebrated the Children's Sabbath!

Please detach and return this evaluation form to:

The National Observance of Children's Sabbaths
25 E Street NW
Washington, DC 20001

About You and Your Congregation

Name _____

Address _____

City, State, Zip _____

Congregation (if not part of address) and Religious Affiliation _____

Telephone (indicate day or evening) _____ Fax _____

Web site _____ e-mail _____

Please describe your congregation: its membership (number, racial/ethnic makeup, number of children, and so forth) and location (urban, suburban, rural) _____

_____

Is this the first time your congregation has celebrated a Children's Sabbath? ☐ Yes ☐ No

If not, in which years (1992-1999) has your congregation participated? _____

About Your Children's Sabbath

Who took the lead in proposing and planning the Children's Sabbath in your congregation?
(Please describe their role, e.g., senior pastor, lay person, committee member, youth group leader)
How many other people helped significantly in the planning?

_____

_____

How did your congregation observe the Children's Sabbath? What activities, service, or events were held, and approximately how many persons participated in each?

Please underline all that apply to your celebration.

1. Focused the worship service, liturgy, or prayer service on children through sermon, prayers, music, or other
   Was it for a single congregation, ecumenical group (different Christian congregations), or interfaith (Christians, Jews, Muslims, and members of other faith groups)?
2. Involved children and youths more fully in the service
3. Led educational programs focused on children's concerns for preschool, elementary, middle school, high school, adult classes
4. Held special outreach and advocacy activities

Briefly describe any or all of these events (use additional paper if necessary). Please feel free to enclose any bulletins or other materials from your Children's Sabbath. We love to see what you did!

_____

_____

What follow-up is planned? That is, how will your congregation incorporate the commitment to children generated by your Children's Sabbath into the ongoing life of your congregation this year? Please be specific.

_____

_____

What support would you like from CDF for your follow-up efforts or your involvement in the Children's Sabbath next year? _____

_____

Did any other congregations in your community hold Children's Sabbaths? Tell us about them, if possible.

_____

_____

About the Children's Sabbath Manual

Please rate the Children's Sabbath Manual sections.

1. Very useful   2. Somewhat useful   3. Not very useful   4. Didn't use   5. Plan to use at later date

____ Section 1   ____ Section 3   ____ Section 5   ____ Section 7

____ Section 2   ____ Section 4   ____ Section 6

What resources or changes would you like to see in the Children's Sabbath manual? _____

_____

About Spreading the Word

How did you learn about the National Observance of Children's Sabbaths?

1. Denomination/Faith Group _____

2. Religious organization or community group (specify which) _____

3. CDF (publication, mailing, meeting, Internet Web site, Children's Sabbath video, other) _____

4. Media coverage (please specify) _____

5. Other _____

How did you publicize your Children's Sabbath events? (Underline all that apply)

1. Print coverage: (name and date of publication; send clipping if possible)

   Community newspaper

   Denominational newspaper/faith group newspaper

   Congregational newsletter or bulletin

   Other _____

2. Broadcast coverage (name of television/radio station) _____

3. Other _____

4. Did not actively publicize the Children's Sabbath

What individuals do you know or what professional networks are you a part of that might be interested in receiving material on the National Observance of Children's Sabbaths?

_____

Name

_____

Organization   Denomination/Affiliation

_____

Address

_____

City   State   Zip

_____

Telephone   Fax

_____

Web site   e-mail

Order Form

Joining Hearts, Hands, and Voices to Leave No Child Behind®

October 20-22, 2000

The National Observance of Children's Sabbaths unites thousands of religious congregations and organizations in speaking out and acting faithfully on behalf of children and families. This year's National Observance of Children's Sabbaths joins hearts, hands and voices to Leave No Child Behind and give every child a Healthy Start, a Head Start, a Fair Start, a Safe Start, and a Moral Start in life.

Children's Sabbath Multifaith Manual

Learn how to plan and promote your Children's Sabbath with this easy-to-use, single-volume manual. Includes practical activities for adults and children, worship services for Protestant, Catholic, Jewish, and other faith traditions, lesson plans, and resources for follow-up activities within every faith community.

Children's Sabbath Video

The National Observance of Children's Sabbaths: Raising Voices, Linking Hands for Children
A 9-minute video featuring highlights from past events as well as interviews with a variety of religious leaders. Inspires communities of faith to participate in the Children's Sabbaths and strengthen service and advocacy efforts for children. $5.95.

Children's Sabbath Manual Pricing Information

Quantity	Price (for each)
1-4	$6
5-9	$5
10-19	$4
20-29	$3
30-49	$2.50
50 99	$2
100 or more	$1.50

Bible with Child Advocate's Concordance

For faithful advocates, CDF presents a New Revised Standard Version Bible with a topical child advocate's concordance. This handsomely bound Bible in genuine leather contains a special concordance with selected verses on parents, children, social justice, and other child-related topics. Measures 4 1/2" x 6 1/2". $25.

Other CDF Resources of Interest

- *Children and Guns: A CDF Report on Children Dying in America*, free
- *Congressional Workbook 2000*, $7.00
- *Freedom School Materials:*
  - After-School Curriculum Guide, $30.00
  - Book List, $5.00
  - Summer Freedom School Curriculum Guide, $30.00
  - Summer Freedom School Curriculum Guide with Latino Supplement $50.00
- *Grace to Lead Our Children Home: The Crisis Facing Black Children*, $3.00
- *Guide My Feet: Prayers and Meditations on Loving and Working for Children*, $17.95
- *Head Start: Helping Families Move from Welfare to Work*, $3.95
- *Insuring Children's Health: A Community Guide to Enrolling Children in Free and Low-Cost Health Care*, first 5 copies free; $2.00 each for additional copies
- *Key Facts: Essential Information on Child Care, Early Education, and School Age Care*, $5.95
- *Lanterns: A Memoir of Mentors*, $20.00
- *The Measure of Our Success: A Letter to My Children and Yours* (Hardcover), $12.00
- *The Measure of Our Success: A Letter to My Children and Yours* (Audiotape), $9.00
- *A Parent's Guide to Child Support*, $3.50
- *Poverty Matters: The Cost of Child Poverty in America*, $4.95
- *A Prayer for Children* Video, $6.50

- *Seeds of Success: State Prekindergarten Initiatives 1998-1999*, $9.95
- *State Developments in Child Care 2000*, $7.95
- *The State of America's Children Yearbook 2000*, $15.95
- *Violence* brochure, free
- *Welcome the Child: A Child Advocacy Guide for Churches*, $9.95
- *Welfare to What? Early Findings on Family Hardship and Well-Being*, $2.50
- 2001 CDF Wall Calendar, $12.95

Order Form

Joining Hearts, Hands, and Voices to Leave No Child Behind

Item/Book Title	Quantity	Price (each)	Total

Standard Shipping by UPS Please add the appropriate amounts for shipping and handling.	**Subtotal of Order**	**Add**		
	0-$10.00	$3.00	Subtotal	
	$10.01-$30.00	$5.50		
	$30.01–$45.00	$6.40	Shipping and Handling (see left)	
	$45.01–$65.00	$7.85		
	$65.01–$100.00	$9.25	Tax (Washington, DC residents only, add 5.75% sales tax)	
	Over $100.00	10%*		
	*Of merchandise total			
	Overseas/FedEx Shipping (Please ask for details)	Extra	Grand Total	

Your order helps support the Children's Defense Fund! • All orders under $25 must be prepaid.

☐ **Bill my credit card**

Credit card number _____ / _____ Expiration date

☐ Visa ☐ MasterCard

☐ Discover ☐ American Express   Cardholder signature _____

☐ **Check enclosed**

☐ **Bill me**

Name _____ Org. _____

Address _____

City _____ State _____ Zip _____

Phone _____ Fax _____

e-mail _____

Mail order with payment to:
Children's Defense Fund
National Observance of Children's Sabbaths
PO Box 90500
Washington, DC 20090-0500
Phone 202-662-3652 • Fax 202-628-8333

Children's Defense Fund ®
Leave No Child Behind®